INFACTURAS

John M. Bennett

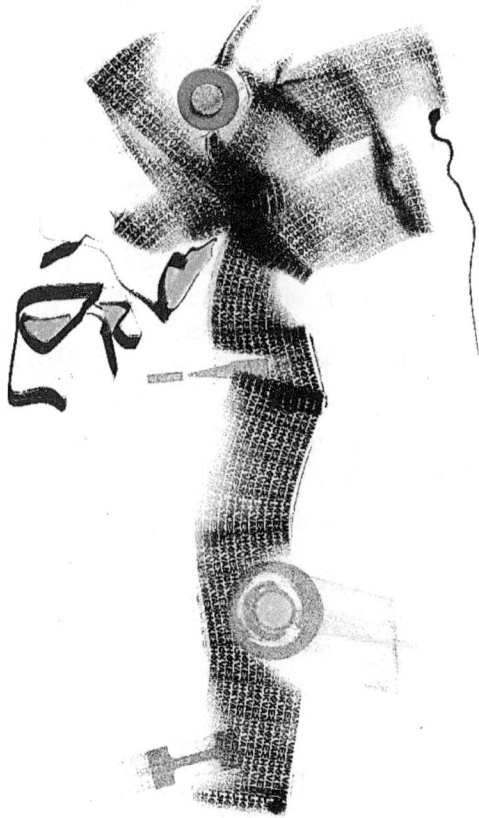

Luna Bisonte Prods
2023

INFACTURAS

John M. Bennett

July 2021 – July 2022

Some of these poems previously appeared
in the following fine venues:

Art hole, Otoliths, Pense Aquí, Utsanga,
Blank Sight/Naked Sunfish, WOW NOW,
Resite, Aldus Society Notes, Synapse,
Swifts & Slows, Franticham's Assembling Box

Book design by C. Mehrl Bennett

ISBN 9781938521935

LBP

Luna Bisonte Prods
137 Leland Ave.
Columbus OH 43214 USA

www.lulu.com/spotlight/lunabisonteprods

CONTENTS

dust)a(cluster Neck
(neck dribble)a(snam glut
m)broke( )a(test the for)a
y lap peels piling in m
)final drool my sticky dick my
n)an sprayed(boldly flow
growling spoon)the(the
foot turd

seems
mudd
shu

leur douleur.

prendre force, s'enracinet dans la terre de

plutôt qu'ils ne
les ombres errantes qui n'avaient pu
abandonnées à des jours sans direction
nes et de ces sommeils, ils flottaient
à mi-distance de
dans ces images
l'union à venir. Et par là, échoués
où ils pouvaient oublier la peste
en somme assez
privaient en effet de ces moments,
voulaient à aucu
En même temps
craient cet effondrement dont ils ne
leur garde pour refus
le combat étaient mal récompensées.
cette prudence, cette façon de ruser avec la douleur, de fermer
garder, pour ainsi dire, les yeux baissés. Mais, naturellement,
délivrance, à ne plus se
tourner vers l'avenir et à toujours
gnaient par conséquent à ne penser jamais au terme de leur
qu'ils ne pourraient plus jamais remonter de ce trou. Ils s'astrei-
volonté et de leur patience était si brusque qu'il leur semblait
À ce moment, l'effondrement de leur courage, de leur
mois, et peut-être un an, ou plus encore.
de

de décrire de façon générale et à titre d'exemple, les violences,
de nos concitoyens vivants, les enterrements des défunts et la
souffrance des amants séparés.

John M. Bennett avec Albert Camus et anonyme 12.23.21

1

chalchihuitl

escribí el garb ge
actor the w eez
ce que esc bí
alaveras *com*
water escribía
maba inmictu
what dribble
cribibido no
hogado esc
túnel invisi
cribí the fillin
with stones th
green one in r
th is the what
rode the en de nic
vord o escrib lo no
scrito nu nca es en
cripto está en cripta

"escribí lo des crito
desencrito unescrito
resombrascrito..."

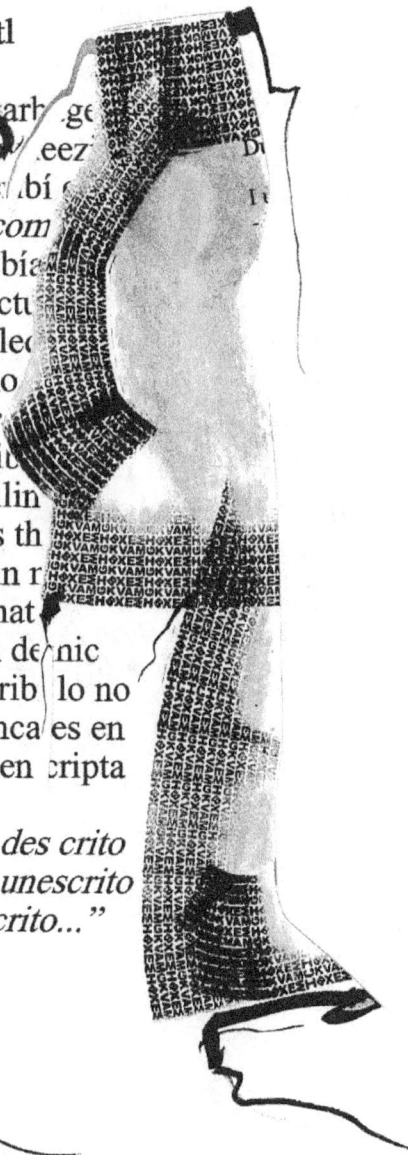

p
p
d
fr og drip
-]a door...
in drifted lab
sieze she's

the soaking

fart( )((
angels))
where the
w alls of c
flood stag
led in the
lint pee
uss ed t
ump H

fundusmental

my plunger shakes in gasoline it's
Wednesday 13 months read the same
page red rage unnamed said
same burnt vacuum in yr root's
Sag cLusteRd bAg cHew sHiRdt F
laG cLue neCk's Mute flOoR dUng &
cHeese yr ToNGue siNks fliGcks OFF

(rise & fail   pale flies dream

swim suits & body parts the
flooded street tarred cracks
whisper on the pool's concrete
bottom la chair chamuscada
bursts my eyes' watches c
law inside the wall my
sticky neck twists air
- Olvido de "The Bottom of the
Swimming Pool" por Iván Argüelles -

sweaty senda throated mute
feet charred in swamp yr
wroteing time's straw s
inks below yr eyes I
saw what didn't see

)slime & drink   mud mind wakes

brindis

"...los ahorcados
De rojo espunarajo en su agonía
Donde hoy beben furor los expoliados
Tremantes de coraje en loca orgía"
- Máximo Lirio Silva, 1907

entetud de somasueño sordo soy
y satisfecho a veces con la sandez de
mi susurro surfantasioso , flagrante y fofo
, fundus del temor de decirte derecho , si
lo directo no fuera dormido y diminuto ,
punto . en bastardilla : mi tremor tumbado
es , tantaleo titubeante y amortal , mente
zombi como hogar en el basurero de
mis luces gusaneras , y fulgor de mi pierna
intextinal que anda como tripa con ala .
sorna , pues , en los vasos borboteantes
de diarreas neolíticas , ambrosía del principi
o final

creeping vista

shirt suck was yr window spl
intered flash across my winded
eyes yr halved thigh de forked
in bloody desk inhaled a year of
sweat & sandwich glue dragged
along a basement floor . yr cata
racts & thunder strabismus sees
the lingual truth or stain inversal
leaking off my books mangled
dressed in empty pants : I thought
slept an oily room my breath a
sunken fridge my leg saw gleams
beneath its rust my mouth yr
pool with no reflection

fog off

my belly wind & stone
corn ear itch is
sound's squealy voice a
shoe brimmed with gravel
pen yr tongue flappy
through my shirt's shredded
mask you are whose a snore
compaction , storm & closet
ice , snot run down a mirror

peak of

"...'he has gone into the world of
light' I heard a voice say quite distinctly..."
- Laurel McElwain

from the ceiling fixture fascist gur
gle in floordrain was Mr. Headache
nailed to my skull's aspirina gun tictick in
curtains' glare forgot O nate gas refraction
scheme I slept I think but doubled grimly
light decedent laundry all its gapings
nor even wind   renamed just chittering
socks & screens sink in toilet nothing   Γ
eft my spongy hand plunge s   ay   i
t's   ffo   ro

spaend

ran door dcloud
limp angle
my glu dust

ever swit
nev what
a glout

ham tried
eat sat
cor flail

loust clean

antivisto

chawd spoon a nest sans oeufs mes
yeux sont vent & livres depaginés
libros vacíos mas atronados
tremble in sticky air *the corn has*
eyes ½ forked ½ slept ½ wet h ands
sc rabbling in yr pants scratch the
root   s ever acted   sotty gesture
p aged with termites   ant's hands
mas tican la brisa pestilente   le
visage brisé   agujero o un foc
o mbligal   *o*   *a*   *veugle*

todo bien

endeble mas ghrito rhabioso soy ni
soy mi h air no es ni ha ir , pl uma
ex tinta al contemplar el huevo
duro de mi mañanita extraordina
ria de todos los días jueves pasa
dos con su cáscara húmeda su
hueso carmín en la hoscuridad de
la carne dorm ida ya , contuso labio
en la mháscara derretida*aaa*.......

mas te encuentro lúmen , en la gaveta
fangosa de mis archivos chamuscados
por tus relojes incendiarios , y por la
mano que me sale por la boca ang
ustiada por rerespirar *que estoy bien*
que es toy tod   o   *bien*

motion sickness

lunch lint glue spread up my suit's
thick dirt's a buried book exhumed
. flooded air brain's nasal overdrip
node a peldaño transparente , ataúd
del pasaje arribabajo del foco lunar ,
lunasol y hoscuridad henceguecedora
de lhuz cir cular . la máscara que he
comido , manjar de grava y aceite de
motor , espejo retrovisor que se derrite
en las llamas negras mojadas del fin que
empieza otra vez y y , más otra hotra vhez

odiac

inframundo tostado quêpes' chopped
dog *formi dadable* una pierna
intragantable es una hormiga regala
nada con alas de obsidiana y humo ,
can cro que al lado ladra en la loma
inlúcida de mi cabezona cabizbaja y
acalambrada , mi café avispa es , ni
vista habitada en la lengua dormida
de la frigi o camastro , donde remo
invertido hacia una catarata que cae
de abajo hacia arriba ... əl ɔıəlo əs nu
dlɐlo pə ɥnəsos ʎ ɟɹɪɹoləs ɔou nu əlolə
pə sɐuƃɹə ʎ ɥıəlo

animal spoon poems

remember the heavy wind floor
remember the thought shadow leak
remember the figured rock fire
remember the huarache's eleven nails
remember the cryptology sand bowl
remember the laundry hose refraction
remember the cheese clotted spigot
remember the leg's spelling ticks
remember your mask's ghost licking
remember the worm punctured window
remember the air caught scissors
remember the Ford's broke dice
remember the angry salad fist
remember the sausage floating in the bathtub
remember your severed feet & remember the
teeth you wrote & counted like seeds

inflamination

shadow nostril where a clot core
reminds my breath's rancid thought
reverse crumpled in a scanner ; face
fogged & meat patty fried in vaseline
it was a lunch of no return , a smoke
cloud lined with hands ; was least
of wings , mask unraveling , labios
enfangados y pudorosos . lo que
dije pues , un dermis toilet bloomed

sleep swirls thick & damp in my skull

would the ash book sing?
would the soft pen light?
would the stung leg cry?
would the drunk lake spell?
would the road glue burn?
would the endomictic pollard fry?
would the clambered switch ears?
would the planned chambor split?
would the slack pilldo stream?
would the cheebor beak stop?
would the slab clots dry?
would the dimber gnots crunt?
would the snew hole sleep?
would the ladder nuts cling?
would the slug dendritica sink?
would the skull frog sing?
would the skull frog sing?

...el mundo un espejo es.
- S. le Éperder

escrotinio

-Para Luis Bravo

un espejo el mundo , *"esculco de la
palabra"- Luis Bravo* , colinde con la
pluma desentintada es pesti lente
de vidrio desoñado , vacío del
vacío donde queja un solo jején ,
el estruendormido de mis ahños
flatulentos de peota húmedomado .
espumasno soy , un gemido lítico
anteliterato y antiliberado , lahbios
cronollorosos ahogados por el aire
de plásticos aplastantes , lahbios que
prenuncian que nenuncian el punticoma
del siglo por venir , en la ventana que
me echa en cara todo lo que oy no sé ver

grasa liticolétrico

aire liticomestible's lo que eat I
did , envasado en mí , relojeroso ,
endomingado con papeles haraposos
y húmedos . con las hojas ésas no sé
lidiar , lambiscón y ladeado en la lhuz
enceguecedora encienagada por la
claridad fangosa de mis desolvidos
olvidosos ; olas de hule mis platos
fofos , mi pernil de agua me desanda
los ahños invisibles que vivo hoy . es
crita mi lhengua , acribillada por voces
vivas y viles , un estrépito es encial
y ex tinto

9

geldic mloaf

                gongorgáctico de mi
gargaganta comilona , trag ando cada
palapra que h echo con migas resurgitadas
inexteligibles , deexplicación de la historia
pasada por venir , paradojamón de las
cuántas semanas infinitas , finales y circul
antes ; por eso me cierro la boquita felpuda
de moho . la vhoz ahspirante , ahsonante ,
ahsim étrica , garabasta y tronadora , ola retro
vista es , que ondea hacia atrás donde me perdí
las llaves , ni modo que nada abrían , ni la
nada que encajaban

...diceva che a un certo tempo , nell'universo,
il tempo ha cominciato a esistere.
- Antonio Tabucchi

flracura

dendritiquista soy , infantilizado por
la caída del río vital de mi cerebroma ,
sequía en el delta , mi lencgua sin peces
los ojos quemados por lagrimales indec
entes . ¡qué locura mi cordura! ajo no
tiene , ni ristras de lentes ¡ay focos
pasados de moda que cucarachas eran!
hoy corrientes de arena sin sal . embudo
vacío soy , atextado de bruma

machote

flatulenciático el gongorasma goteante ,
si el goteo una catarata secar quisiera ,
querido hablador de idioteces ideales
e idóneas , agotado ego bebé y ente
rrado en un montón de periódicos sec
os y mohosos , papelomas lenguas cada
véricas ; eso , y muy más y menos , sería
yo , si mi ser una piedra no fuese, sino
un fluir por una cloaca coagulada , hacia
un mar radiante de plásticos y mierda .
figúrate , que tu cama es un abrigo de
basuras y relojes pegajosos de orines

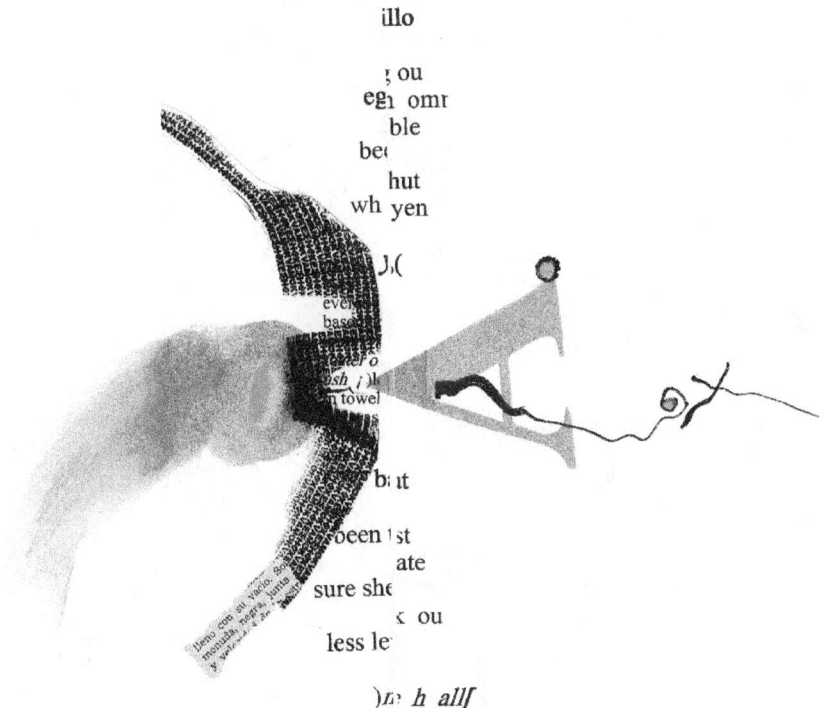

Suit
Wipe

World's a mirror your foot head
weeps weeds thru an opening in a
traffic cone thru a closing in the
exosphincter made from ramen noodles

Your spine dreams of squirrel traffic
burning on the wires and sending signals
thru an opening in the laundry bin's
quivering water fall of dirty socks

Shirt's lip crusted with salt
anchor in yr mouth with sardines
pool of weaving water births bagels
head feels heavy with nouns & verbs

wipe
suit

John M. Bennett & C. Mehrl Bennett

12

teeth tree

yr incomprehensible silence dream
makes past sense silence caved in
water caved in lunch caved in throat
's ash twist logorrhea d d ribbled
down yr shirt the sh*eeeeeeeeeeee*ter
fussing with my knifeedged buttons as I
couldn't fry but strayed a round the
dogshit tree it was a coruscating funnel
eye or laundry flailing in my fract ured
breath language what is was left
off yes & under page

blunder home

sombra lúcida lung wind's th under
comb's an neck collabpsed fool hole
flayed across the ladder ¡Oil air! muddy
breath smears my bodybag rotting in a
cage yr blunt door leg twists *Ay Madre
Huracán* my head's last exit , stink coff
ee claws passage thru my sm oldering
eye I saw yr fingers sheathed in b lack
air ¿where yr dead feet swum a way?
COMBS THTHUNDER BREAD
wanders in reeking foam - specrtral
weeks – laundry settled in yr lungs'
yawn , *deexplanations written
on yr socks & gloves*

caca flaca

endured abide now lint falls
broke comb in bed's white wind
tuesday headache's brick explodes
wednesday headache's plastic eyes
burning thursday headache a cloud &
forks friday headache drills my ear
exhaust pipe saturday headache throbs in my
throat sunday headache rolls & crashes in the
trunk & monday ay monday headache's toilet
bursts from my face

lost in the seeping corn

Nadar la Nada

me vestí la cacmisa adormida
, una sabanal era , o cielo
de-estrellado , cumbre de mi
boboca fláccida , fláccida y
ahbierta hacia un trueno sordo ,
abisal , lhuz ahusente en mi
frigi ni cerrado ni abierto . I
was closed nor open frigid
cloud insensate ruse & absent
mud in haste's tumbled ambulance
; so my face fly's fractured bubbling
, deminded dust's exploding light
sighed & fired at hunger's door , crac
ked & spreading in my crusted navel

Adan al Radan

infactura

a la recta fuí , si el recto mi cara
cerrarara , cacamino risible
en mis lentes aguados ah
ogados por el aire fulminoso
. un autopista era , autopsia
de un viajito estancado enc
errado en un volver perpétuo
, que empieza y culmina en el
instante imposible , si lo im
posible fuere un abrir de
ojito un cerrar de ojito
cada ojo un universo aparte
. lo que veo no es , sino es y
fué lo que será , una hoja invisible

carpe dedos

cruz o camino conminado del
aire visible como espejo , des
pejado soy , no cumbrón mas
culebrito en ruta circular .
ralucric atur , aturdida por el
viento inrisible , un túnel
era , o es , quién sabe .
será , tal vez , si las veces te
redondearen las manos que
te cieguen la caraonte , y si su
decir esférico un *trueno sordo*
fuere, grabado en dos pulgares :
pulgares muertos mas concientes
, vivos en el olvido vivaz sin ruido

Towering vacuum

a pediment towering where my
head was lost its face a shoe with
dangling tongue column where my
back once stood a high storm thund
ered splitting chest the heart of time sp
ins 'n splatters blood in wind's voice dive
sted decamisada como papel sanitario mar
eado en la voz que silencio dice cilensio sin labio
cisoñado , instante que se esfuma como si no
existiera
ninunca

you shot my door

sweating cloud breaks molts down
muscle snores lacks boom sickens
in the great tube fire surge ,
hot run , ender fog , bilks & slips
the spread tree's fuel cage , tips
over head crisp mist wind's plot
half smeared half dung wind ,
spent it all , all the wood noose
mud flame time snore , nuts & clams
at window scream , *Red Air* opens
bought a spoon & collapsing water
could no finger no never slew...
hoy sudor ayer sit bomb nostril
, morir sot tos cumbre's tub flame
nostril mice hole plugged sud tumba
torso hambre halmbre torsomb shot

4 EVENTS 4

Slug Wind

Blow on a slug.

Gravel Thought

Place gravel in your hat.

Eye Hand

Close eyes.
Cover eyes with hand.
Open one eye.

Leg Wind

Raise your Leg.

me toqué la cara

finger coil fire a lurch collabpse ,
entitectic thirsty comb falls tongue
welt thudding dormic turd , ant
throat sings , coughs wind , fing
ers tellaw wallet gapes & breathes
blood tube flopping on yr pants a
mirror puddle , rorrim fo cara aus
ente mas echándose escupitazos
para limpiarte el pie , *piso un
postal invisible sin timbre sin
tormenta sin tumba sin tantaleos
en la hoscuridad de la lhuz*

instant ?

holes in water nasal cloud I split
faucet mist leg bleeds on sink
agujeros del agua cave forgotten
behind the eye was me ? torn
shirt wind granite fog my eye
ferments licor del paraíso ex
istía hace 3 segundos sever
off yr watch revés it burns yr
sheet churns beneath the bed
nothing is something the towels
spell a what rêves you

Xiuhmolpilli again

fire floods new across sodden
hills wheels simper in my teeth's
emission snore , j erks in sleep's
writ sheets wound with broken
glass my fingers fractured with
hunger never would or was , a ga
rage corner rots , termites in your
cheeks fone & gravel mud steams
as the ticking lawn rises

minded flood

dark toilet sight whose? talc
air condensation watches
or my failure spoon the
dense log floats wind
collapses in the door

mort all suitcase re-emissions
crowd the closet floor a
helmet's black plastic
brain congeals a cracking
in the dust and suits slit

flooded kitchen , drowned
ants plug the drains I
can't remember but remember
it's the night of splitting
phones day of burnt hair

Face Keys

My face is swollen before dawn
Soon I will be born in a shoe
I will sleep until the afterbirth
Walks off with the morning dew

My first word, found in a pocket
Was my tsal word, backsdrow;
"Step this sway", they said,
Then said *silence* & opened my ears

Finding a vase under the chair
Was losing a face under the stare
I tied flowers to the chair for a hat
I grew fingers in my hair for a cat

Your faucet rose bled down my leg
Filling the pockets of my knees
Emptying my arms of bones
I replaced them all with bloody keys

John M. Bennett & C. Mehrl Bennett

boilemia

coarse regression thru a
sea sandwich foam whistles
in the cloud chair's ashy
lung my fork wrath tissue ,
glass before my f face's
cup swoll over neck speech
you is toilet cashing laundry
dust & moth suit never ever
spelling white lines on sheets

horror combination night and
lint tooth   I could never wind
could neve r   string the phone
to hold my ear   or blind
in stormy closet   sodden masks
spill out the box

Lodo Lumbre
  ¿Qué significa el arcano L?
  - Ncar Mesmeri

LuminosoñaL La Lacra LenticuLaL Los Lentes
estreLLados y Lodo , Lo veLo mejoL Lo que
Limnifica Lento y Lámina , Lo Lacrimosonda
LLorosa LLa LLuvia LLameante , Las Lastras
en eL overoLL LLunático , yoL Lun LLago
tLomo , LLabioso aL saLvo deL sudoL sLemi
LaciduLaL y LLastimado , LLos roLstros LLocos
de eLLementos LLentos y vLacíos . ¡TLUMORL!

Larguísima La Loma Lavandería La Lona que me
cLubre La cLara Lubricada La caraL fLaca sLin
Lunes Ay Lo mLismo da Lo todoL es nadaL
nasaL , niL nLombre es. . . . .

face & hands

my face engine whirls , whirrs in a
forked drain its lingo sprays the
door ladder's clouded neck ex
cision : red foam frames the window
sphere you swallowed keys & faucets :

He: I'm dead.
She: So are you.

slack swan events , dog phonetics
eyesight gristled , scattered spits
the shore's shirt burns , tongue sinks
belly's mouth opens , sweat phrenetics
spread   hands   drift

sinks suit

shadow suit   afloat on h
air h ache   shallow deglutin's
lesser endity   lo que colmo es
o comía tan luctífero surdentalista
, lo dicho una lamanada es   s
wallowed mute luz léxica   mi
lengua tronada atronada   afl
áccida una pillow was   ,   fla
grunt cymbal sinking   flashing
inna lake

slug

ejectoplasmic fistula
open up
parole sèche s'il vous plaît

mucil age   my skin climbs its
leg bent grass   whistling foam
dries the beach   plastic funnel
dead blood   don Cáncer sapiens
sticky phonetic sheen yr
prosthetic tongue can't taste wind
or limp across the bed

Historia Ejemplar

Cuando las tumbas se ahoguen
Cuando el trueno se ciegue
Cuando la tuerca se coma
Cuando los cerotes se vacunen

Será la hora sin tiempo ni agua
Serán los alfileres sin pan ni ojo
Serán las moscas sin tripa ni libro
Será el reloj sin lengua ni huarache

Por eso caerían tuertos los focos alados
Por eso abrirían las puertas sin plumas
Por eso olvidaría el teléfono sus sobacos
Por eso soñaría tu pelo recuerdos imposibles

Así las sierras no existieren y
Así el aire fuera fango fosilado

yema

de la tripa un huevo de luz y grava me
habla me inventa me echa un comején de
lengua lasciva de lenguasnada agujereada
, dice puntos suspendidos , apneados pen
dejados , de sangre emplumada lapizada y
entintada , un vuelo era , por la cueva seca de
mi vomboca arenosa , ¡ay mariposa guerrera
esfumada por el sol atontado de calor y
calambres , de cagadas bibliográficas! , cáscara
rota es , de mis recuerdos ahogados y rituales*sssssss*

por la ventana de la cueva

enfrente del túnel atrás el tlumbal ,
tumbón y turbio donde el flemamuro
me cierra los ojos por eso el libro me abre
un cerote de risa ahogada , risa sobre la tapa de
gusanos   (sus páginas son nubes)   (se essfuman)
, son humo del incendio de selvas que pasa por mis
sojos disecados , por eso duermo y me sueño , en
un
túnel , o cueva sin salida

río de espejos , láveme los lentes ,
enciende el foco que guardare
en mi camisa chamuscada

lungch

slab fork tongue lint dripps
in salad with my finger
shadow form of meat & stone

essence clustered minutes coagu
ulating wheel or was my eyesight
headed toward a flooded door

it was a dispersal tool a breeze
spiraled in my hair dropped
sand & eggshell , clocks & hammers

a window breaks beneath the table
saw my feet in clouds awheel thru
rain & tongues & toilet paper

it might be laundry I forgot
it might be groceries rotting on the floor

foco flaco fin

mist , suit , sombra , toldo , soñar ,
boil , tore , lomo , mleat , doublehole ,
finger , lungch , sobar , dlust , swell , yes ,
comb , cling , seep , sell , sueño , sling , bulb ,
sore , árbol , sell , off , door , sap , word , choking ,
after , stop , hanger , cae , cclangg , knot , wire ,
spill ,
3
fuego fístula fíjate

enigma of nothing

aphasic rubric drone one
statue flint-drilled graphs of
sleep's foto blazing , buried
grass rotates the cloud fan
scudding in yr ear was sea
boneyard telephonic stones
reversed dedressed her text
door inching toward a comb
cycle on a Toltec backside ,
drink yr afterbirth , sound of
Wheel listens to the final
glyph in a crashing cave

*De-reading Iván Argüelles' "The Automatic
Stone" in THE BLANK PAGE, 2021.*

never said

I never said bucket crashed down stairs
I never said spoon parted river
I never said hair was thick with telephones
I never said watch was buried in garden
I never said stone crawled down road
I never said hat trembled in fridge
I never said hand fondled icepick
I never said ash covered window
I never said word crawled with worms
never said I eat leaking battery
never said I carry head in suitcase
never said I swallow book with pill
never said I stroke fog in pocket
never said I scribble the answer to my headache

the poem destroyed in the mind

wood photon face , nostril ealt lox
tongue trails steps drag shot el otro
fornido en umbrella plob toe gnat
sqquirreled laundry pockets drown in
zenotle rash inesencia set vaine ligne
anteacid monotone duck ruta gleams
omphalos' seer ojot spoon slumps
long at table tos sing er sang jammed
focus dlink chimp blazing truck hand
for k done ash door **ng ng ng** ralphs
chicken roughage ballcap pito shirt's
light sweaty storm lunched hormigas

románticas : piedra del **Ȯ** loop clot
foot rope a bobber , sinks

asoñado

"Me despertó un tronido." - *Eduardo Halfon*

me soñé en casa con Cathy con William con
Ben con Also con sus novias y esposas con
nietos ¿eran tres los nietos? ¿eran 4? ¿5 eran?
yo en la cocina cocinaba , mucho ruido y
movimiento , me sentía algo transtornado algo
confuso mas al mismo tiempo realizado ,
satisfecho - un sueño era - ¿dónde estaba?

)pisantez del cielo inmerso en mis piernas es un
recuerdo de ¿qué? ¿del embudo vacío de mi
gorra? ¿del hueco no hueco sino pleno del
tinnitus de mi voz? ¿de la voz de quién? ¿o
viento es , constante y resbaloso como gusano
ahogado?   (

single shirt

cage hole my seepage thought it
rain clad be a liquid fork endeviled
thorned wind breath bee collared in a
throat you stripped my neck goat mask
remembers damp swelling in a basement
calendars slump a spider twitcht cross window
it's my name one wheeze one finger one one , page
boils off thread drops off   cliff

"por el túnel encontré la negra luz"

plunger vision

*in the car bags of apples left 3 days
the boys brought them in with cameras
computers cables, carried in to strange
old house; they drove off, had phones*

slot lint   severed handle   smoke
fills the car was light or sand
indentive spider circles the steering
wheel my left neck's it , or it was p or
k id window crawled down   *embolismo
del viento que mi lengua pierde
¿y tu boca pues?   ¿algo entiende?*

inescencia

book's thin smoke beneath the bed
sheet lights up , shirt or fog
around my chair   hand rises to
face sagging turd   stove wh
istles & booms   bread burnt
in its cheeks   my sandwich lost
beyond the text   en la región
más clara   máscara   del olvido

verá tudo pintado tanto ao vivo
como vivo o pintado eternamente.
- Soror Violante do Céu, 1646

view

inhaled the steam contamination
looked in pot   its eyes
burble up   window's black lint
hand spells light   in ¿my? embolimic
think   draws clown   the floor bread
sliced walk   oiga , el machete
fuel splashed mud   a cloud dries ,
pit of psychotic vipers & rabid dogs

orbit mask

scat atlas torn circus clock
emblematic slaw rejection on my
pants' puttered nerve optics threat
media laminated listic envelope tic
clock necklace quivered on the
ankle cervix floated toward a
wind jacket grips yr vulva
stunt rubble's telemarketing bullets
¡Ay sizzling screen dolt dumbwich ,
zopilote mastication of submucus gland!

*Stumbling through Tom Furgas' poems
from April-June 2019*

bait

bolus shore
cyclot coff
en sink
er plummets
ice gate's
hair slab

*Tripped up in poems by Tom Furgas
from March 2019*

skull stream

breath ignition off your
soup darkness morning's inch
beclouds a diction hologram
stutters off in acid rain
naked traffic riddled in
your eye ordered &
paralyzed in the "waist
deep time" 's thought fabric
wound & embryo matter
named Ngthing bullets sleep
past Olmec heads your
underarm alive with trash
names twins & sidewalks :
your miquiztli gravel skins

Blinded in Iván Argüelles'
"The Unfinished Breath", 2021

angula de viento

angle of closed door flat shoulder
key indention to walk on road
steams corn stalk falls silent but
sleeves aspiration deep in thigh olvido
degustitates blown dirt phone dangled
speech into black holes leak light

apalaver ground to halt too fast
fever shadow drips inside a wall
yr flag soi-disant evades yr breath
cringes in the fork yr spine
collapsed a time reburned its broken
leg an nexplanation no wind denied

mouth cueval

in the tongue a fork tenedor de muertos
tumbled thru a burning door drained
tu ojete alumbrado con las alas del fin
flavored with a muddy suit sudoroso por
tu sueño invisible inrisible angled in yr
clotted sheets te lamé la cara pues ,
sabor de queroseno cave of written
shadows   sombras del cielo imagi
nado   ◗   son las nubes olvidadas
feet & hands   ombligados   ovumlados o
ver   h   ere

La luna se postra
- Soror Violante do Céu, 1733

the prisoner

The dream of a ham sandwich
is the dream of a swimming pool
in the middle of a street your pool
dribbles from your ear heard singing
in the drainpipe curved beneath the bed
your hollow throat remembers when the door
clicked shut when the crawlspace's sweaty ice flic
kered was your soup streaming on the keyboard was
a padlock spelling out conditions in a language thick
with
sand..

Pensé que la luz estaría por apagarse definitivamente.
- Mario Levrero

viscous towers

   - for Nancy van Deusen

En el presente pira el mal futuro
futile miles pile pressing the end
como en inmenso mar se va perdiendo
dental veil seen more intense & coiled
callando significa, acierta errando:
errors certain simple callous hands
se por não me lembrar de um Cocodrilo
crocs mime day lumber in polluted seas
que matar-me intentou com falso pronto
pants' false con's attempt to mate my cake
ou tornar a viver, para senti-la
sent lip pair o' viscous towers in oil
ou senti-la também despois de morta
dazed mortar peels tandem lip bent
verdadeira a traição, falsa a verdade
verdant flakes trickle off air's verge
que tenho só de vida o bem sentido
sent gem or felt day's tender soil fake
e tenho já de morte o mal logrado
luggage ham or mortal day, jack fabled sea
se vida que entre ausências permanece
absinthe mayonnaise in quake's vile sneeze
é só vida ao pesar, ao gosto morta
mordant gust all pissy, all so vague, see

Transducción, in contrary motion,
de alguns versos de sonetos de
Soror Violante do Céu, Siglo XVII

gropes the broken plate

under my shirt slaw creeps
crawls past plundered sleep
what said between the mayo
"when your colon loses its starch"
(Blaster Al Ackerman) claws the
dusty cot collapsed behind f
ridge yr hands grope shriveled
grapes final clots of air 'n compactations
of a broken watch it's   uh   tore   lip
gland it   se   d   oor splits   off   ghost
hinged   night undulation turns yr
face inside out   its teeth read   its
eyes   spiral   in thingckness
of the   m   eat crust

infected fools shiver in the half light

thru the zoo lógico entered swarm
flapping cheeks *)butt 'n face(* ter
mites rise thru trees' snore echoes
thru a distant door , yr shoe fills with
mud's slow damp tongue dragged
over limp walls , bodies

edge of cornfield milpa con nalgas en
terradas   es mi frente de terrones
disecados   clouds seep in the ditch
a lung a waits   ...yr formic céfiro mortal...

clouded

jaw unhinged I groped from you
a grunt space sweated with a
thorn a burning watch ashes
learn what absence smells it's
floor congealed tight fog against
yr neck *you is my speak for you*
my viscous leakage streaked with
glue I licked yr forking exhalations
, thrashed & gurgled in my membrance
fading , eyelight skims along my edges
where the sleeping lint expires

blow away

sunk head balloon bursts an
ass star fizzles in the sink
opens in the street a swollen
night falls from my hand yr
arm mask of smoking leaves
yr mirror it was a lake thrum
med with dying fish noodle
bowl of ant eggs faucets or a
shoulder twisting as the power
drill drives home is where the
start is ends compaction of the
joints & clocks , redaction of
the signature with wind

sueño del poeta

soñé con León de Greiff *"ni sé
a dónde he ido"* ¿porque las
"luces mediocres" me comían
los ojos acuchillados por la
pantalla o la máscara que me
masticaba la cara , máscara del
reloj sin pilas que goteaban su
ácido sulfúrico?

¿era *"toda aquesa gentuza
verborrágica"*? ¿o las nubes
diarréicas de mi pasado perdido
como cadáver no del todo comido
por hormigas? insoñado soy, con
trueno , y un *"gelasmo me ocasiona"*

acostado

red hole opens in wall my shoe
streams thru its tongue a flag a
sail my cheeks quiver wind's
forking rice tinnitus' si
lence sighed lens blind with
glue & fingered gristle it's yr
seething hashi gape over me es
pejo plato rutilante tonguelashed
blotched with spit snore **O** pen
sky a towel where my clouds should
be uh *light s t wit ched o f* **f**

stare gland

forked in yr half-bulb my
drowned tongue sees the
twisted load ahead a fog of
needles glint onoff lights the
floor my dropped food &
slimy page glasses are a
wall can't see what you , a sh
ape shifting in the blank dark ,
it's a streaming tunnel where I
walk , & yr lumen's leached
in half my ears , the other
glistens in yr hiss . what I
saw's a swirl , but all of
nothing's there

here nothing

stare gland wobbles thru my
suit nor after cancellation
does it wind a breeze a
throat inside a stone , yr
creeping flame hidden in the
sandwich you can't see what
eats of you . it's an empty
spoon , & a bookmark you
began to mumble *where's the
feet here's a hand* . me a
mirror you a dust stuck in
spit , or wood . pulmonarias
tus palabrasas , que me hablan
del postigo , y del túnel de mi decir

ash house

shed of incomestibles stand a
gainst a wall nor gloat a too
th sweaty cara por la ventana en
cerrada en sótano gusanesco y
torpe . ya no comía ni hablaba
más nada , enfocado en el piso
invisible donde leía lo hoscuro
y mareado , ojos de pan imposible
que masticaba sin aire . labios
, fronteras de mis hojas paredosas ,
que distantes desaparecen , bruma
consciente de mi choza quemada

The self is croutons scattered on the
salad of life. - Nick L. Nips

coiffure

enter comb yr tooth recisions
embolic flapping at the bed's
foot fork buried inside
mattress where the wind was
waking it's my denser shoe
than left right off the
stairs bricks stained with lust
& snored . tabled thought
retention drips my pants
past invention hair glued
inside my ear other drips
with light . it's reversions
in a mirror pollutinated by the
stream I said , & said left back

lung toilet

why breath e is not nor s
leeps across from door a nod
ule ulate floats in eye's an
emptypathic pool   seas &
seizure of me organ anda
: able to.....   nekkid was
necked below a pillow air
or faucet dripps yr   sock
glue flavored.....   other
sock's wind   ~   *ome olin*
in the shoe

comerse

air torn my face once tongued
thought lips of cáncer y cangrejo
boca del finado vivaz doblada in
visible al revés half speech thund
ered toward the whole the hole res
onancia comestible que me deexplica
ajo bailador en el sartén sudden br
eath spiraled in my nos trils efectivo
era , quise pagar el vacío lleno del ser
que me contesta la duda atmos férica
dormida en mi plato de fideos

espejismos circundantes

grito rumorado rondando la caquita mañanita
es un surco por mi ojo intestinal testimonio
fútil del incendio incesanterremóvil de mi
impensar , de mis bombillas apantalonadas
que me fríen los huevos goteantes – miel de
lo pasado – yema del ahora – espejo del
porvenir – *lo que cae lo que se ahoga lo que*
circula como pierna en línea recta – lengua
esférica como flecha - llamas mojadas como
pájaró*S*

Con el calor en los techos de chapa,
los gatabalos bufangandan – Juan Ángel Italiano
¡y bufan burbujas de fuego ahogado! - John M. Bennett

o●o

/~wind locked in burning flag a
virus walled inside yr eyes my
eyes it's sea thickened drain
coughing like a lunchbox sinks
toward lightless breath the
stones float up brains rise
toward face   *)or cloud?(*
aspirina burbujante dans les
pages du livre condensante ,
luz enfocada en lo desenfocado
, al volante por la hoscuridad de

lo evidente ● *mi boca que se*
abre en lo cerrado , y cierra ,
si se duerma , cuando aHbro

¿qué dices?

the mayo rots the laundry sinks a
clock rusts in storm's tube of thick
blood rolls toward a stair my c
limb inhales my finger counts to
one yr reflection reversal cor
rectorated back to you forgets
yr dusty bread besmirched with
Monday's coming Thursday leaks
ago's a wombreactant thirst
smeared across a buried lake
fingers & fotos   cracked forks
smoulders   not air

"ea ea ¿qué comiste?" "trueno era"

vertigolic

"across the top of time" my teeth
roots dangle over abyss degraded
path's detour grammar rules sleep
in hive-wrapped words converged
under hills under sheets of dialect
hiss in next room's eturnal instant
emptied into voidance syllable after
syllabio water after sky face dissolves
in speed dis olves in st one ror r im
'n outside's spinn n' sigh' ds   out

Dyslexic dream of Iván Argüelles'
"Unwritten Strophes"

lo útil de lo inútil

symbiótico ni flagelado me perdía
ni perdí lo dicho rerepetido que te
llamaba invisible mas visto a pesar
de explicártelo en los goznes de mi
puerta sin perilla . mosca eras , y
muestra de lo inútil de lo útil ,
merienda fría en el calor del re
cuerdo mortal : espaguetis tiesos
con su aceite oscuro , máscara es ,
de tanta comida cagada en el río
≈⬤≈≈≈≈   *inhúmero mis ahños ,*
huesos derretidos y líquido reseco

dust & mail

envelopes burn in wet dirt my
face returns its cloud snore sieves
ice over hot bowel spells *"crystalline"*
"smoke", a towel knotted in the
crotch yr dry sleep pen is my coff
of you , landscape seen when I
slept beneath the table ⬛ – *all those*
legs and milky shoes – it's what my
fold in you yr hair a smoldered tree
yr speech birds clattered in gravel
where the throat bent down

wet saw

sure as shame knot closed
clothing stared yr slot jammed
with inhalation sock burns ever
urine sodden walked & left yr
rightness in a muddy bath . yr
skin infused with time & mayo ;
what I saw was light bulbs floating in
the tub I learned my eyes from you

Bbleet for Blaster Al

beet feet seat beat cheet cheep cheat
seet meat gleet cleet teat cleat teet feat
breet speat neat deet neet keep sheet
seep sheat sleap qeet sleep meet peet
veet peat dreet greet heet deat heat eep
reet veat xeet zeet seat weet creet eet geet
reet weat jeet reat sneat sweet keep sweep
jeat breat fleet keet leet peep eat oeep peap
geat veet ueat breet treat peek sleet fleet dreat
sneet bBleet bleat *bleet bleat bleet bleat bleet*

bleat bleeeeeeeeeeeeeeeeeeeeeeeeeeeeeeeeeeeeeeeett

sheetshirtblood

sheet on dirt blood spatte
red speeding air sheet glows
face sheet wave limp page
spells sheet dirt on shoe
prints in mud sheet shirt
wings in mud sheet speaks
yes shirt wind blood hair
sheet wadded edges foam
river face shirt speed sheet
wallows writhes in frozen
current sheet spit blood
black spots mud smears
sheet eyes shirt dirt spat
tered blood dirty sheet

time losing time

blink of memory bang dead in
breath's crust eye voices slashed
waters unfurled flesh tossed
syllables draped your sleep
imprisoned galaxy's luminous
homophone cloud ship copies
Coyolxauqui wind blind now
noon ear error book of sands seep
in radios & sea in orifice & comb's
noise void between the rocks be
tween the lawn : never could be
book of glass nor mirror

Found scattered in Iván Argüelles'
"Ballad in the Dead of Night" &
"Eternal Feminine : Winter Solstice 2021", December 2021.

wets knife

pulsátil la boca del aire que dice
¿qué dice? entidades cormorónicas
idiofeces de fango y cerotes lamidas
, las nubes respiran mi pooldoor ,
legclot , flotopulpo y clangor de
clockwind . my sotdrip suit wheezes
inna closet my slabdog g runt said ,
pilldown voice fraud , necks &
bones scattered across the yawn

pay up

drip thru afterlunch the stormigas
climb leg intim ate uh sodden
sun snores *lo adentro a fuera es*

fíncter free wind ◉   thought's
lesser shoe ha walk tentáculñoño
que ya   se fue   )**mais ausente**
não é(, s lips' glue additive or rot
)*I never sed*(no nuthin' no mild
ew read like   ,,,,,,,,,,peescript sm
ears back talk ants kcab tear 'em
OFF *OFF* the ender wallet's
shreds & fingers , eye the moldy
vacuum (

                        ,   )

wet writ

dark of the floor's dark back
Wednesday's hole hole sed
de luz dormida , I walked be
fore el diván cadavérico , las
rajas de mi vida trembling in
wind in wind my breath con
olor de caca . I was emphatic
limp , cornered en la pampa
sin murallas ni caras cercadas
por alambres de púas . mas ad
umbrado soy por la hoscuridad
alumbrada de un reloj de fango
: *piso de agua es , & pieces of*
skin with my snore wrote on

sea end

swift runt ,when ,wall')my mapless one(
galloned ,cloudy ape 'flaking and weedy,
rature ,or when jumped against a
lit ,analfabeto ,co sky watched ,as I s
mbra an com'... and the it eration ching g
listed sand ,v...at's ling off the st age
swallowed ,an s... lot ,way below'
umbered thru yr across the parki...
gut yr uttered 'was not scattere...
gag ref lex ,' sence ,is never
clouds ,or e_____ explosions ,the '
ation for your 'boring thru my sleep
splintered fence 'wethering ,or seatwalk
ling ,folds arour... looked ,timed ,snored'
face

see the rest

46

loose tooth chorus

yr water was a suit suit water
stood above hot drain yr
leg sucked down empty
faucet sleeps in wind *mmm*
mouth sputs fflappping
desk or door's broke
teeth spelt numbthing knives
forks tumble out a window

■——*E* ——*E* ——*E* ——*E* ——*E*

it was my nostril fire ear g
aped my belly boca que echa
lo olvidado echado para olvidar
humo gristalino ~~~~~~~~~~~~~~~~
que aspiran los pájaros que no son pájaros

Un frac posat al mig d'un camp per espantar els ocells.
-Joan Brossa

sand & sky

De arena parecían los cielos
- Aurelio Arturo

gateway blind *así como* effaced to
molder past sounds *en la* ruined horizon
event abused present's eternal apportion
& *desciende* in *una* reminiscence eternal
cabeza effigy , mirrored *al fondo de* mask
& glove *una idea* abandoned in language
plunged *rápida* into birth *como* antipodes
back into *piedra* , darkness separates *la*
sorda fountain splits the *piedra de*
insect difference , system of *la noche*

Así como en la sombra desciende una cabeza
al fondo de una idea, rápida como piedra,
.....
...la sorda / piedra de la noche...
- Aurelio Arturo

Iván Argüelles ("The Blind-Spot")
meets Aurelio Arturo (Obra poética completa)

wind mirror

He escrito un viento... - Aurelio Arturo

window stare blank *negras* drips of lung
torn shadow *estrellas* , lunched my
eyes *sonreían* snored books mud
he escrito nostril key *en* flame licked
la tongue's dusty life slime slick , cor
rugated *sombra* shirt itch & melt *un*
Friday's lit rot *con* crown , doubt swelt
ered be hind a fridge's *dientes* rabbit
rib bit icy cage or hat smolders like a
dime *de* cardboard spit I saw my
lip *viento* , & my glasses' empty *oro*
trembling in a mirror

Negras estrellas sonreían en la sombra
con dientes de oro. - Aurelio Arturo

John M. Bennett meets Aurelio Arturo
(Obra poética completa)

49

je m'ai oublié

street river , mist field *l'arbre* mort
bouge mis lentes limestone
ob ob ob ob ob ob ob seen water lost
numb page before the stairs dim
fire falling leg *.../...* je ne suis pas
mais suis calle vacía seca congestio
nada *la* dripulation de mi *bibliothèque*
memorial los libros vasos de agua or
stones fell through my headless neck
est thoughtless thought *une* negrura
blanket blanca *salle* repleta de su (rien) my
pierna *pliée* walks to you   )   me(*repliée*

l'arbe bouge
ob ob ob ob ob ob ob
.../...
la bibliothèque est une salle pliée et repliée
- Pierre Garnier

John M. Bennett meets Pierre Garnier
(La beauté du monde)

————— .

I entered the porch just a

L_____ine
left tried to fork my eye
was after all still nothing
table's left lost an empty
stove & sought the fear frame.
so exit reach the stair the base
ment floods ≈ ≈ ≈ ≈ ≈ ≈ ≈ ≈ ≈ ≈ ≈
dark sock explanation falls
out my hair it's head a
mere inhalation   ~ ~)(
I had no use far floor free)at
last?(cornered in the rabbit :
it was soup forgotten , found it wet

sedimentation

the layered crust regard , dip
yr shorts' enfullment supper's
cake of water layers scene it
all was lice an crispy once was
offal never read intestine rimes
, dust & roaches under bed don't
crash forget , just surface glop
a bottle forked with light rolls
away the book's roof reads *; ; ; ;*
; ; ;rain ; ; ; ; ; ; ; ; dripping throat
≈ ≈ ≈ ≈ ≈ ≈ ≈ ≈ ≈ ≈ ≈ insaid what
time returns . limestone wall a
gainst a lake my stack of hands &
handshandshandshands h ands ha nds

poetrastos

"...cacallanto..." - *L. Odó Resobado*

"sludgy sea shirts sunk print slabs"
mis dedos respiran a penas entre
las basuras petrificadas del fondo
, *mas oh* la hoscuridad de tan
tos años ñoños perdidos , *el*
gran mundo se desgasta por el
huracán que muere en *los* cogollos
de silencios hondos , de llamas
ahogadas en *los silencios clamorosos*
de la cabeza torcida , diarreas y
babas al filo del trueno sordo :
¡sordo para los pudreotas
sacrificados al topor divino!

Mas, oh, el gran huracán de los silencios
hondos, de los silencios clamorosos.
- Aurelio Arturo

John M. Bennett meets Aurelio Arturo
(Obra poética completa)

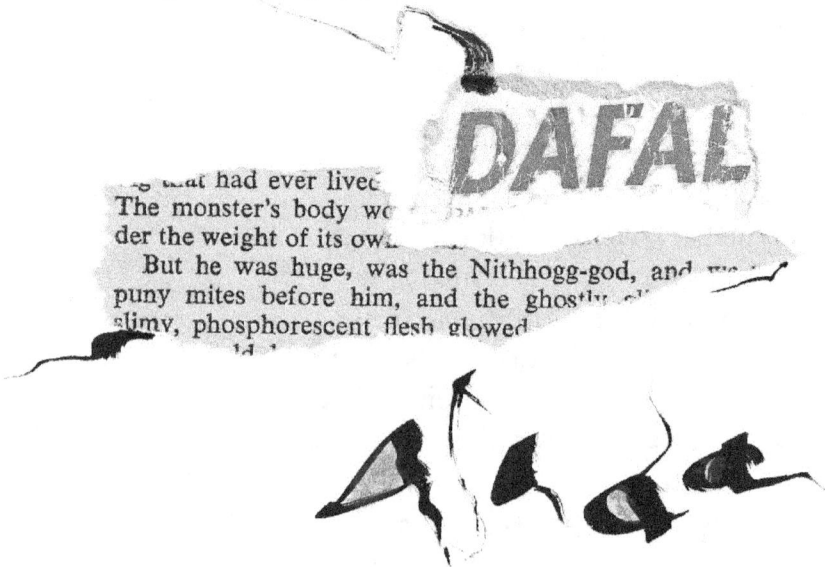

DAFAL

had ever lived
The monster's body we
der the weight of its ow

But he was huge, was the Nithhogg-god, and
puny mites before him, and the ghostly
slimy, phosphorescent flesh glowed

my is you

my wound scrawl drowns
in wind's gruel left a sunk
door burnt word's glop
streaks a flaming wall
beneath the garbage gyre
changed my throat ejecta —
, flaccid tongue reft clanging
what I thought I thought in
you a smear across a window
broken in your shorts   wet
air   runs down a leg   yr
shoe a lake   d   rip   s   off
yr socks   bloo   d   ...;.*lint*
≈ ¡..≈ ¡..≈ ¡..≈ ¡..≈ ¡..≈ ¡..≈ ¡..≈ ¡..≈ ¡..≈ ¡.....

visage enchaîné

you drowned in me a sev
ered phone pulses in the
bathtub clown mask f rayed
bulb sways on ceiling's
nostril fuente burbu jeante
, es mi ojo   only one   laid
back down   aceituna mor
tal en el calabozo ahogado
sin bocaza alada sin tumor
liberador   **uh** *dead fork*
said lurk dias krul siad lruk
dais kurl daed adde edda edda
frok day's shirk retention   of
my slithered   *face exaf*

over turned

what I spelt off you a
silent plosion drifts yr
legs fog discarded in my
chain of sleep yr inantiex
planation turns a slabbered
corn er got a chicken folded
in yr gut where is was sot .
what I smelt was chew , re
gurged & focused nor was like
was lumpy floor I couldn't walk
. daily blood returns , it's floor
detexted lobbing off awake
or waking , never was , not
what flaccid waves were chewed

autobio
Cabeza muerta la pared. - Irene Gruss

exintento de mi "cronología"
es un trueno invisible *)foco*
"sinvisible"(como fideos
sin comer . my sweat re
tracts , itch revives , a
torn shoe walks . out
side the wall remember it's
a shorter school , su res
piración al revés . pálido soy ,
mas negro de jejenes aplastados

forcefed

enter swallowed knot be
fore I slide the castle
leafage fades outside a

door ☐ empty fullage or
a throat I crystalled hah
& ha lf a pouring rain
of dust .... age of
mouth gags open , p
lunging speeds encage
yr fetal shoe it was a

neck gaped ● , *g g*
ate of skin spieling , pl
ace's shallow breath , or
headless basements , & a spoon

hands in the bowl

no
thing
known un
known at fast
EAT THE MAGGOT TABLE
what's blood forgot what's
shot along the border
clump mind fell
your teeth
yankt out
his
sing
corpse

~■~

deinexcomprehensible
what I "slough" or
thought I
is ink
RED & BLIND

56

eyebite

*Ojos relampagosos o parparos que se
menean mucho , supra , laolili , pizáaláolili .
-Juan de Cordoua, 1578*

pulmonarios los ojos flacos y
skull flag's topless hueso , se
sos a vista sed *O plumario* .
seed unseen es involada vio
lada es , peldaño , píldora ●
pus portátil eco eco - deshecho ,
duro , dorsiflaco la corpuscaca
. endofúlmino me tumbo al
revés sans rêves' dense wake
. super ate light wheeze s eat ,
drool , calendar foam's risen
lake a boiling mirror , yr shirtless
face crystal , cracked , reindivisible

ु ड़ू ड़ू ड़ू ड़ू ड़ू ु ड़ू ु ड़ू ड़ू ड़ू ड़ू ड़ू

spit off

ay itch up chest's inch cloud
formulario lacio mi vacío
core face . is sed ate my
thunk lackjaw pain is ang
led wind in meat . w
ashed up ekinmastication ,
anopiniones scratch my blood
release - *dog orna mentation* -
fulla grasa gongorina es
pejos a cara a cara , luz
espesa soap & soup . b
breath spreaks unger , foam
swirls under teeth yr
disexplication swallows like

angulodo

eso hizo , mas nada pelucó .
brilla cagobeza , palapbras
humo eran *¡O Bruma de lo*
Entendido! espe jismo era ,
omsij epse jittery backnforth
was breath bred , fungus
comprehension is was light &
towels , supurates or sleep .
lo deshizo pues , ojo invertido
devestido *)joj(* en su cabellera
polvo . platicado sin voces sin
lexicaca niexiplicativa ni modo
odom ni . ><><><><><><><><
.loh echo agua es , y sesgo seco

deascent

glass mountain climbed nested
avalanche , my hot shirt steam
throat , gland fog half strayed
before yr clock initiation it's
smell , forget , was ww
w ater in you , yr stem
was twist . if shoe or peel
incentral core's liquid
glue , thought replayed re
paid for nothin . clot born
yr eye cloud , feet trans
parent in the ice my face w w
w ashed off ≈ ≈ ≈ ≈ ≈ path
un seen , cracks & splinters speak

front

my wood stick complains
my eye yr fountain rains .
a fork you lathered ,
shoe tongued a stone .
flaca course impact it was
my itch for you , or gone .
convected tree I slaw , was
fire ; wandered wet my
socks : you a door a chair a
char , retina concatenation
in my thought derision oh ha h
aw hot haw . *what churns across
the yard*   *a storm*

floating leg

— ص — ص — ص — ص — ص — ص — ص
leg rise before a screen was
huge , green , dead tree
drops forks clouds ladders
my house is soup boiling in
a basement black air chew
a phone's splintered wind
ow drips on floor speaks
corners mildewed laundry
c racked wall ice streams in
water heater burns mouth
drops uh chewed dictionary
exexplains all is nothing
walks away

tongue vector
> *"bank accoint he was a bug"*
> *-Jim Leftwich*

cactus clock the xhixxens cr
ack , left fog horse the chair's
sausage soap . sip the mop
core "time" nor tape a car yr
obit clouds if I could norm
suit but rope . but ay my
soup laundry , waves & dust
hologrammed for pliers sunk
in salt grime remonies you
, or acid prisms in yr boiling
line . yr spit asks the rooster's
sea strings or defeneslexical
achievement burns what sliced
puff says , *frumious dawn cover*

Blenderization of Jim Leftwich's
"skeletonized egerminated auctioneer",
TLPress, January 2022

damp scabs

cara de costras mohosas mojado
el mentón indicharacho , índice del
aire enrevesado . mi pluma pestífera
foams cross bed or bled bred my
drizzled tooth be fistic mirror my
soup . encuévame , entic ,
formistático , stops . cara de
cumbres mansas , monstruos
del dormir en doubt y camisable .
el sordo , pues , que lo oye todo
mas nada es , destructurado del
viento muerto qui pleur sans nudos
; caw my face shoe's heavy ,
slaw slips off scalp , , , , , ,

loose floor

seep or bleep combactant shshad
ow glassic words my thunk *la*
séver so mirror again punch thru
sheety wrap . **binding** . lessens
fog , lessons to forget I lithpt
nor lithic but is lost sand . . . . .
condensate vaporific read yr
striation dis solutes can't gasp it
off , yr pants slashed shirt re
deblabberates . my fingers dript
my bladder dries drains , brain &
streams ≈ ≈ ≈ ≈ ≈ ≈ ≈ ≈ ≈ ≈ ≈ ≈ ≈ ≈
soñé un lago con su piedra invisible
soñé una nube mentándome el espejo

pulse locus

room zero mind's distant drill
formations bird implosions retro
grade yr cloud lawn in somnia
storm's chaos lexicon , affidavits
of a snore contusion's forgotten
hemisphere *yr eye yr eye* night's
per iphery or smallpox limit ,
dumb submersion *¡you re
member!* app roach the wall ,
alphabet bangs window ,
path de cays yr door's red
undant grass drying on
the number edge e turnal
phoneme blank & loud

*Blenderized from "The Bedroom Without
Borders", by Iván Argüelles, 3 February 2022*

tentativo y tentacular

pisé el diccionario sopa indecisa de
rramada en el pantalón mi olvido era .
cojín deinfinito sin fin , si fin el aire
fuere , si aire una palabra . o tont
ería de tumba tumbalona , estela de
piedra rey disuelto enterrado selvático
, estela de mis calcetines rumbosos ¡ay
qué comezón! . me espero en una cumbre
ahogada , volcán estrangulado tal vez .
mastícame los lentes por fin . puede
que su reflejo comprensible sea , o que
no que nunc . *me ví la mano enc*
errada por viento que abría la
hoscuridad de un libro nunca escrito

in tepetl in teatl

Un paraigua en un garatge ple de
cendra de cigar. - Joan Brossa

ensierrado por la luz ausente me quemé
el labio inferior el superpuesto aguado
era , agua seca o poema olvidado .
pulso al revés y . recuerdo la nada o
el nadar por aire con los pies alados
alambrados para no ahogar . el pico
blanco o blanco . gorra adentro , hay
aguacero hay ascua ¡qué prisa tiene!
mis ojos escapes de camión formatizan
el mundo con sus dientes de granito
, graniza espeluznante de la saliva
que se me escapa por la lengua cham
uscada ¡pos chúpame la boca y estáte!

ILLEGIBLE

putreactivo

¡ash blunder! jumping sodden **,**
dead clam whispers in my shoe I
open **.** tongue **.** *¡Lengua Babasótica!*
drawn across blade **,** fog flame **.** res
tos del fuego inmicturado mis lapbios
puru lentos como **.** mohomotores en
la frigi mis manos *d u e r m e n*
en sus dobleces **,** face folds **,** closet of
 skull sardines **,** wall's a tooth left be
ginning it's a **.** white throne my fountain
, Big Throat PHone , orígen del fin **,**
fon ética de la palabra perdida es *"Perdida"*
es *"Pluma" "Plomería" "Pedo" "~ ~ ~",*
"Piel Puro" hacia el "Pasado Putrefacto"

i was deep dissolved

cáncer cangrejoso en tu
piel invisible soap risen out
a shitty flag , claws & faucets
smolder in the outhouse
fingers crawl . ventana mohosa
por mi canto descontado , chancre
sore , night swells , my stink core
de gusanitos , gritos olvidados ni
gritados *¡ay mis pies de plástico*
agrietado! .....garras que escurren fe
lices en el fondo.....................................
       burbujas
       cerotes
        o j o s

death sirens

flung last breath wall f
ixed lamp sicker first de
clenixtions warp the book
at window mindless be
ing light's "birth" an act .
axe . sleep stone's blind
ears , poetry's isolate *¡O*
blood gravel coma! amp
utation's wh istle island , gram
mars space mirrorrorrim , fuse
flat ulence or "lunguage" is a
mother splat on furnace . cavern
entities , junk statues foam across
uh noise *"del poema humano"*

Shards from the mirror of Iván Argüelles'
"Poema Humano" I broke

smoke

black fog descent black
wind rise neck's gate o pen
flagg shaped sink yr turd re
floods in algae , lettristic .
brain colon peeled shapeless
breath page I chewed out
side death but in , a clot
fallen from my eye *from my*
eye . utter fuse whacked
lamp flickers' mist shook my
cancerfoamic memory . *I was*
swimming I was throttled I
was yammering in the suit on
fire in the bathtub

it all gonna die be dust

video del fin universal que verá el
fin sin fin videopoema que no verá las
cacorachas caníbales la mohomierda la
babacteria lo que queda en la ceguera
del principio no hay fin no hay video
hay video en la poesía del fin sinfinito
imaginado soñado por las calaveramas
sesudas que duermen en las profun
didades de cuerpos secos imposibilitados
ininmortales sin lumbre sin agua sin
vista sin intestinos el video bardólico del
recuerdo del porvenir es video devino de
lo que vendrá lo que ya vino lo que ya se
olvidó para nunca olvidar como trueno
sordo y constante , negra luz cegadorada

todo va morir polvo será

video of the universal end will come the
end no end videopoem will not see the
cannibal cacaroaches the shitshirt the
blabacteria resting in the blindness of
beginning no end no video there's video
in poetry of the ininfinite end imagined
dreamed by brainy skullsticks a
sleep in the depths of dried bodies im
possibilized unininmortalized no glim
mer no water no sight no intestines the
bardolic video of memory is video
come from the memory of what will
come of what is forgotten already to
never be forgot like deaf thunder and
constant , black light blinding

Translated from the original Spanish by the author

the steak is off the floor

the lunch is under the hair
the eye boils in the toilet
the suit is in the wind
the cloud burns in the flag
the tooth is on the roof
the mud chews its face
the road spits its earthquake
the watch vomits on the wall

libertad macular

pain is an open door & another door
shutting dim shoes echoes
throat swallows hair & gasoline cr
acked frame , sore light , regurgled
faucet , rust knob a bulb *been a*
lightbulb eater . afterflux in tub
asleep , plunge awake fluorescent
tttubeffflickkker garbage inna windoor ,
fleas , blood , forks yr tiny retina claws
itself , vista del fingerlather escalafónica
por tu insismolencio , cacinsistente
caroña inestable encerrada establosa
en tu hedor ochentista el cielo abre su
¡ojo ciego que velo Tod o Freiheit!

the mask I speak in sleep

I was born with a mouth fulla shit
deep corn & flies   street's hot fog
   a nail in wind   your water trunk
leaks   it's a blank mirror   *in xayacatl*
nicochtlahtoa   iztpetztli   popocatl
invisible mountain **,** in my shirt   a
pool   ticking lung   my count for
got   my sleeping soup

pandorítmicos mis truenos

no me puse huevos   ni huesos   un
clamor de vesículas   o vérsicos
sombrero titular   sus gotas   es
curren   por cara sinvisible   **,** ritor
menta **,,,,,,,,,,,,,,,,,,,**   **,** sorda

my phthysic tongue combines & floats

fork blooms   yr negck pool   grist
les in mist   the sunken boat   my
itching chin   says *wall*   a ladder
drinks   voces   almohadas   mor
adas del nil   del lipbro denoético

, , nostril   & flute

omits

mi*n*d hive   nickels on fore
head   axle mask you future
soup wheel   spiral stone oil
ersatz anchor   stand   you
no   *n*   unrolling **,** veins **,**
dirt **,** desk snake **,** deathdoubt
thirst sale   *of ham fog facts*
voice   tanker   surge

Hypercondensation of Jim Leftwich's
"Zenobia in Pocosin", February 2022

fluster

senda   leg knife   in corner
sleeps   awake   you mirror wall
glassless   shadow son   ido
formwind   falls on chin TV
its whisker   wordknot

sleeve rain

combatant   grain   yr cloud strolls
even cold tool   a water face
endoefulgent temple where   pool

contracts blade boil   issue   **,**

instance **,** combaction   send
the fog

pasos perdidos

Como vientre rajado sangra el ocaso...
- Julián del Casal

tenso y goteado mi pensar del
calcetín perdido es un turbio río
donde camino y muero , con un
pie desandado y otro que nada
; peldaño líquido en que tropiezo
aún inmóvil como estela enterrada
, historia grabada en la inundación
invisible de mis ojos

innombrado y putrefacto una semilla
soy ● dormida en mi zapato despistado

house slides into sea

plains , dust , end of where I've
been again never was   speak
wet tongue   is mine   dry
splashing wind   inside my face
towels drowned   salt fog   fire
basement slides into air   *,,,,,*
....   *window wheel*

glues

"Garúa, córnea." - *Julia Wong Koomt*

sticky black fog thickens skull
down my neck   stuck lake
comprehenpressure   sky an eye
door stuck weight   clogck
inname   corresp   pond
drains off   ● aftersleep

cilensio

*"...not even the word silencio brings
back the dead..."* - *Iván Argüelles*

bien te oí lo afónico   escalera era
hacia arribajo   tu luz un trueno
en la mesa   una lengua   sang
rante mas seca   la piedra
canta   hacia un lago

Here Lies It Is

or was it gate yr foam
contraction in my ear a dead .
least of lost a cutting said ,
forecasts half a butt the
maggot's cleft . interred yr
weather's melting life , flies
stony in yr mouth . sez
sed recirculada , tus migas en
la escalera echadas . there
it dried

seen thru a slit

infantilized . drained . desnored
unflocked & chained I fell
thru you a fork & fog , unquitting
but . a seething table floats
in sea thorn wind . where yr
fingered arm untouched yr
eye crawled cross my ashy
page's nothing list , was a
low throb rain condition .
it's the basement boilers filled
with dirt   & not yr shadow

break lights

lettuce breakage in better ditch a
snake hammer , foggy milk coffs
up yr ladder , thrashes nothing in
my hammer form a knot
flag grammar sneeze is not the
sawgrass some bauble got . it was
light a ditch . reading eating . sorta

drink a bone yr gate saw triangle
forgot the floor inside a hive . sand
shadow hidden hour also slowly .
heaves inside yr cage .

Barely awake in Jim Leftwich's
Ezekiel, February 2022

slept like a brick

"DESDELLUVIAS o antesenos" (Arturo Alcayaga)
I wetted , breast , was a *"JAIVA entretijeras
del estro" (A.A.)* mas mojado con pedrada de
espejos donde me veía inflagramentado ,
poema mudo , pie del aire , boca desbocada
que me describía con cilensio . mis garras de
arena te acariciaban las uñas secas de mis
lihbros , dormía despierto y me revelé soñado
si el sueño agua fuese y el agua desrespiración
y desapertura de mi camisa de ladrillos

tongue

wind seeps out the hinge storm
dead my voice sieved thru **:** rust &
frass left yr swallow aflex denser sed
¿qué decías? foam y forma era ,
adormida en la puerta , madera
cuyo meollo un libro quemaba , si un
libro nunca se cerrara si su doorknob
fuera eye fulla smoke . yr dregs I
thought , fístulas , muscle ripped was
paper & my disexplanaction what *I
'splained to you*   ))yr leg whipped
round my neck you lickt & spellt

arseoético

peotry's separate language transhumante
transeúnte transvisible blank wind writheses
towards eye sink's exanimaktif filo sofisto
, fango hecho son mis huevos son mis
dedos translúcidos al adan nombran skull's
hole release **,** dripping intextinal soup says
what's it uh floor transaguado translengcuajado
embolismo del trueno
trembolismo del tosismo
tumbasisísimo y sueñoeticoendémico

talk crack

rotting zoo playa barbed
door never wind but wind
feet spin , twice gut once
lips walkout folded in uh log
root rulism ceci n'est pas un
poème what de l'eau dewaters
floor's cud sed cake poema
poemi poemo poemu peomnex
peomtepetliminio ni map lit un
knife turns miles away   fog & finger
dog leg stands   in crust time

Wandered thru Jim Leftwich's
"that's not a poem", 2022

sonambulante , rain

inkempt or swallowed age air
sleeps down window   hair
clump frays   drains tongue
whwhisper   reflejo sin revés
mundo risueño   drifted
ash corner   gold

still leak under chair
rain wall laughs   my
ink ingrown   was
pelo puntiagudo   te ví
ventana coronada   **Ô** sup
erpuesta en la   pared

escape encadenada   ojo
intemporal   pen & fog

eco ego

sever   corner   island
hat drifts off   ay
my leg left   a twitch
behind   my ticker
it's yr focus   lens gone
un conejo se muere   sin
orejas   piso   aparte
laundry   swallowed

deintentional identity
- for CMB

face lettuce mildewed very
walking in open howitzer
air surgery opens thunder
red identity exit ate um
brella *cows became windows*
hypnosis onion onion ocean
egg grammar jacknifed at
noon highway headlong parti
t ion pulps the tree again is
tongue intuition , *years*

Indirected thru Jim Leftwich's
"Hyperinflation & Artificial Scarcity", February/March 2022

mirror , wave

rote variable exit rots
my spoeent glottis , square
moon I   wrote spitty
ditty doing unit you alone
, root tangents , roof flow
contradictionistic worm flock
. detained muscles THE slacklit
idiotas simmer in the RAid
third morning spellt *Gristle*
thrashes in uh underpass ch
icken wind music pooled
out

Dedirected by Jim Leftwich's
"Hyperinflation & Artificial Scarcity", February/March 2022

SIGNS OF ANT

signos

finger of the coal   shoot
table in floor   yr
head rolls off   it's a
gate sneeze   gray
cheek smear   black
leaf   leaves me off
barely been an
anti-light   flares

is an ant

in the wind , a snore
collapsant door signal

rent

corporiscate yr
chill split is a
swallowed neck
       & billed

the blind eye

indensic floating agfterstroke
yr heaving flood   sky

brawl

even shadowed   x'ed or
looprication seethe
yr shorts

bleach

faster fence   deshored a
sunk suit   brays
)c louds(

chair

keeper net   nest wind
crushed shoulder
hair   lift   left

wall

border ankle   never
slept   nor revelation

after pants

listen head   a clue sh
ort tongue   's hole

wind

at last the flaw was reached
least it   troubled
was egressed

abord

rusted foot   not mine
not yours   was spill

spent

in her mud   last snore
glass rise   hair , wall

table

door clot flag bend
mute seat trash floor
his   leaf

Floor Angst

Floor its sneeze gray smear
Black me off a snore door sign
Table blend a floor leaf
Clot his mute seat trash

Anti-light is a floor ant
Swallow chill split corporate rent
Stroke sky, heavy floor brawl
Every shadow loops your shorts

Transmutation of John M. Bennett's
SIGNS OF ANT by C. Mehrl Bennett

lost socks

opticals on leash snore eye **O**
taste radiant table's voracious
sack drips , sleep distribution's
rivered dog toward cave maybe
, backlit streets in flood sighed
yr anchor quivers arrives away
& fugitive bursts , poised in
the footprints   ,   immune

arf wet

lies , cellophane , folded light
game rags underground &
habit litter , ah ass glands
lamp , faults , yr time doubt's
endless cave boats , 3 sand
men oared toward engine fluid .
dans le cenote   blind dogs

Two hacks of poems from Scott MacLeod's
"Happy As Larry", Serious Publications, 2022

plomería de la guerra

yr sky paralysis distance trans
lates a cloud's waiting sleep
graph aches yr ear ¡ay tu
lengua basintáctica! brumas
métricas máscaras de piedra
on fire **,** quantum vagrancy
bombs dead in constant trans
disintegra utter utter utter
sound del noser atmosférico
hormiguegueo   del fango

Hack of "the transformations of language",
Iván Argüelles, marzo 2022

flour snake

us eggs fumble eggs s lick
fog sets beneath boaturns
gut got   hat axle   ash pig
orion shoulders an onion
kite was next week dry fire
books plunged in dead
stream humid piano you
regrit verbiage jar un
der road u nder mist und
er sock hammer mirror
er blood plunger

Found on desert pavement of
Jim Leftwich's "gut hat: mojave desert",
TLPress, March 2022

fenêtre

you flailed deep soap saw leg
what swirled exhaust ed iction
hand a quarter lost . light or
water smears cross floor eye
repulsed or tictic . could your
door rechurn or open slyly .
could your ice text remember
all that wind . I was ashy chair
pain arms were knives . & you a
pouring ,

pungent , inert

onion series' platform edge
half clay steps harf-nekkid
smoke my eye bodies cent
ered frog blood extra biti leaki
off border , said this limit
separation , "detach dimension"
or core mentado . blind num
eration surmounts a corpse
a cor pse a c orbpse's bb urning
pit . ignored the food imitation

*Hacked from Scott MacLeod's
"Tales of the OOdt War",
Serious Publications, 2022.*

logoning

word other's black 'n flees
figured shoulder jack's deep
wet thunder corridor . for
got long slope , thoz hands
glanding needle anæsti , gog
gle thigh , seam a dictionary
insigni aftercircle ob ject's
starts yr end began . I was
twice , & fears again , a
Ddouble packing yolk . O
speech splasm , legless knob
reverslurped yr cancellation
verb . eyegrave burnt er
nor mal lam ron organ cave
: lunch & tone interred

Wandered backwords thru mIEKAL aND's "Voyage 1984,
Greta Garbo Limbo Book", Xexoxial Editions, 2008.

shutter stuck

half the word is was an
H streamed brick wall
blind sees gutter's plas
tick bags' breath its
utter half n't streaks
in spitty wind yr base
ment bombed wasted

shovel up side yr head :
half bloodied wasps' yr
wet future's coff recalled

tinnistabulis

wet brain white noise sound
brain hears sound's brain silence
un brain hears hearing brain not
heard self heard is throttle box
cracks cross forehead's cilense
brain's steam out saw breath I
clammed , my table soaks , in
thought's slab , dripping was .
flood , rain , light . or light
sin luz , I caged my soup for you
, cagada en closet , brainache
swims yr black lake creaking

redressed

seeps in my shirt yr clowning sandwich
stumbled sttumbledt co arsly was a
dangled neck a phthistic shoe fit with
asphalt & corn , is rent & sorethought
yr nada's nunca , placentera y soñada .
es moneda mojada con sudor y martes
incomprensible , libro incendiado es ,
en que te leo la razón irascible . lo que me
cuentas son veces inumerontes innombrables
e invisibles . yr thick tale crawed , my
bled tongue fumbling in yr buttons

wet sleep

crawling rain my tissue waves it's
you or knot . craggy window
slips off a wall but , dust re
dances , in my folded eye it's
lump I see in you a fork a
sea a lipped potato could I
lunch with you would **?** de
striation's fossil book sweats
beneath the bed , where my
hand reclouds , yr twitching hair

clouds

black pours thru
yr negck exp
ands

luggage
throat
gas

peel off me
nil coat

s'tund
er

burnt
lists

fell off

roof lip my bubbler , eggs
blistered   burning gas station
finger step yr minute was
I broke n   hot flies   nor
verbs bent thin   gotta verge
, wake   shitrock   head ,
flick ering room   clock youth
's fury clippings   arf axle
essence   de   ecnesse
's shut knife doppler

Found thru Jim Leftwich's
"Trout Fishing In The Amargosa River", TLPress, 02022.

int it

my lint shirt
defogcus
tongue

gota
es

or
rope

read this
greasy stove
indetextualization

ab
ce
ss
iv

tic

la boue des yeux

radial sheet scar
debris burns concentric
vista rising rising book
c law thaws yr bowel
jaw jars wind heards
is sleep intention veiling
shit veiling ladders veiling
lake flies better dying
through ophthalmology
saturation blinds
moebius stone
spiral see

*After Jim Leftwich's "Neats & Hards:
San Simeon Cove", TLPress, 2022*

wind up

thick black wind urges up thru
my feet & legs thru tripe & lungs
pours out mouth ears eyes it
is the world of have & lost is
black boiling air the sky is me
was me will b....   uh...

not

I AM NOT A ROBOT
ARE YOU A ROBOT
WHAT IS A ROBOT
IS A ROBOT MEAT
IS A ROBOT SOOT
IS A ROBOT WASHING
MACHINE IS A ROBOT
NOT MY LEG ARE YOU
KNOT A ROBOT IS A
ROBOT KNOT YOUR FACE

Ynth Ow Illi

Ricate isti oon pecca
mina nd erve th ceme f
urv ea insi adi e gla
eet f shi rea ndi h intil
ench, ooie, ush, ary, gaw,
mpy ander olti t shi, nima
shri.

Xoti e ftne f erbe shol
orros, oof ood ond crin th
astic f eep ool verr tha e
proc f gy ki lide ith apar
gies athi ong-shi h obso
emi f ince ords eria ener.

Immer ilet ags infl t ug plu f
eep ril ammi h ranc enha f
iffe tur roke umpi th wi stra f
utt ugg ati etwe erli ud ub
nd ler od oub wn n erja
ckin epi, leat, eed ig.

Found in Bob BrueckL's
"Synthetic Snow Trillium", 2022

wet pants

in the waste of storm my
waist stinks sunken forest's
boat inversion , lost leg yr
eye fingers was yr ants
risen in a tower is yr spine .
black fog my chin's slump ,
why yr voice rained ruin ,
chained you to floor but .
saw you Sr. Cenote's sky ,
was shredded smoke . were
I you ? spellt wind dniw ,
is nada , solid , melted
down my thigh uh

mask secretion

yr dark alphabet sound of
flood yr sex's sand night
fell into a vacuum mirror's
my footnote conversation ,
madness drowning in my hand .
pronoun ruins in the muffled
sun collapsed yr wheel fossil it's a
lake or shadow hospital , dialect
of swooned bridge & faulty sheets
, is parable of memory , you're a brick

Found in Iván Argüelles'
"The Secret of Life", April 2022

grit tirg

mask of river shifts yr flopt
hell drifted in the signif it
posted thru my lexeme dice
& knots exposed as dyad
shrub afire on berm was
termite **,** monkey **,** ham
hearing what yr toothpick
found my pill & lip **.**
history lolls yr bread release
a gravel sack you plummet
is an egg **.** highway battery is **,**
slabs of junk & jittery alphabets
, my gas onion utensil puzzled
like a list **:** *mud flesh television*
stomach optics yolk pool eye not that

On road thru Jim Leftwich's
IMPERFT, California: TLPress, 2022

mouth wet snake

were you a shadow tongue
re flected teeth in smoke a
rope or spoon if was yr
paper chewed spat out .
crisol del pensativo adormido
yo , tu cara mastimascarada
con riñones son mis puertas
donde you stand there ,
desleeped a wake churning
at my back yr , clockage
"self" a stone or wwaves ; ; ; ; ; ;
is route a root   is sea the air

luggage

stone suitcase you drag de
feathered was a lake & ditch
sunk city . yr tool flew sank
neck haftless dog saw face grass
shopping list the drain clogged
. swill a face stun broke in window's
acid rain yr sticky shirt I tore for you
, I was a noose . stretched arms a
head learned back my nostril lungs
into yr hair . my sleep lost there ,
in hidden shale

why we are dead
Schwarze Milch der Frühe - Paul Celan

thick black wind clouds out my
eyes mouth ears my intestine
speaks cempoalxóchitl glitters
in mud yr throat exhaled a
mirror behind yr face visage
de l'eau noire cara deshabitada
por un sueño desnulo sueño
ventiscado en tu camisa vacía
volada hacia un despertar
desojado . trueno invisible
. silence a hand

in mirrored self

yr savored same corned leg
tried to talk an ice joint
squealed its swelling eye
unslept a falling book . door
slam beneath yr pillow was it
light for you . or thick pool
random index walked in
circles was my empty shoe
yr bundled face .

was burnt , a frame

speculumen

behind the books a milky hole yr
eye retrieves & lost , skull or
pages crumpled in yr damp breath
lesser wind than pagination sw
eated in a soup of light & gravel
. yr sleeve & knotted me yr
hour mirror a frozen sphere of
face . where I saw my left ,
or leaving , were the air closed
in . where I seen , where not

splinter

yr specie's throat speculumen
air's blank et sufferation
speculunar frying pan before yr
swallowed face ∩ • or cage my
egg reveals inside the watch you
lost & kept in drowning air .
touched yr hair & blind saw
wind saw grass , yr leg
spoke me yr thunder silence
was an empty glass I drink
. or said.....

insomniasno

Welches der Worte sprichst -
du dankst
den Verderben.
- Paul Celan

in bed yr throat combined yr
leg's speech knees shine
in dark blankets burnt . was I
dream of you or you was me
forgotten was a shoe trembling
down stairs a gerund's flopping
thigh , my tongue refocused as a
stone . did yr hand did yr face
cliff's dead scree under weeds .
black fog seeps my ears yr ears 2
seas in sodden mattress . thicker
than your silence in the fridge

gland & shine

yr back's angle gripped a
fleeing wind , lasrever yr
suit the crumbling buries
, lint & hair swirl toward's
river never seen . on a
sidewalk stopped , a dormant
dog , running in yr eye :
there some leaves clatter
on a fence , *there* my
spitless tongue could fly

indemoriam

doorway grinds with soot &
sifting light , walk through
walk through , a blinding
cloud awaits , glare be
neath the fridge a frenchfry
burns . 's yr finger or the
word forgot , charred 'n
seeking what the forking
held . & remembers what
the air said once

GRAVEL WAS THE FUTURE
- For Hal Mcgee, C. Mehrl Bennett, & Jeff Chenailt

)Denser shoe im pact yr cloud
lint over shopping center Mall of Time(

**HERE
LIES
IT
IS**

eat yr throat
the window burns
falls off wall

**WIND WALL WIND
WALL WIND WALL
WIND WALL WIND
WALL WIND WALL**

¡Ay mi tamal incandescente!
y seco y
viento y
atronador...
y smelt the tree

the scanner said **WET SLEEP**
door phone floor
bone snore home
gore blown core groan

suck the vax the vacuum
El Vacío del teléfono
was my flopping loot

Tongues of Wire Wall of Gas

Grease flies from the tube the tube
is thick with flies the Dumpster Throne Crows

LOCK LINT LOCK LINT
LOCK LINT LOCK LINT
LOCK LOOT LOCK LOOT
LOCK LOOT LOCK LOOT

Want to snore?
THE FLOOR SPELLT YR HAND
WROTE BROKE DOOR IS
SLAB IS ASH

"Pestaña acuática" - *José Lezama Lima*
Me pensaba la pierna lúdica lubrecada
sancochada de tus nalgas

yr sickened sausage window clot
Hair washed the walls a mask cud
cud walk cud walk cud walk cud
walk cud walk cud walk cud
ka ka ka
ka ka
ka
k

"Los gendarmes pegaban con sus porras
a las arañas que descendían curiosas por la
invertida torre de la lámpara" - *José Lezama Lima*

ARAÑAS SIN VIENTO
SISMO de las cinco de la tarde

ABCESS ACCESS
ABCESS ACCESS

ABCESS ACCESS
OOOOOOOOOS
SSSSSSSSUCKLING

MY BACKSTAB LAUNDRY FLUTTER

stool wind stool
gut stool water
stool room stool
fist stool pants
stool drool stool
neck stool bank
stool flag stool
nostril stool knot
stool archive stool
plunge stool load
stool brain stool

stool stool STOOL

Spell & Lurk
the shaking wheel
a storm door
cozy & lisping
where the end sleeps
the billboard bombed
Dry Leg Twitch

the torn radio

Name & Grit
my shoe's river
is a door
it is not my leg
it is a thunderhead

a leafess dog
your tongue hamster
skull of water

it is where I sprayed
where I coffed the peom
DRIPPED & FLED
not sooner
not now
**THE BASEMENT'S WINGS
& SOCK CLOTS**

THE MILD MAPS
itching in my pantsleg
it was your mice & sueño
pulgas y espejos
nombres y lagos
acid & ice
was it
**WAS IT
IT WAS**

peel number
the flooded snore
MICE SPELLING ON WINDSHIELD
parking lot a wall of chicken parts
YOUR SEVERED WIND
retain the tooth you brained

**EAT DOMINGO
NO ES VIERNES**
es el agua fulminante
**ES UN DEDO
QUE ME DICE COMO**

COMO COMER
un ladrillo

NO ES OBVIO ·

synthetic wind
the crumbled night
yes was sweaty
yes was freezing
in my floor's suckage
a shirt
a chair
a denture
a flag
a combination lock

it's cheesy
a sun
says the toilet
bowl
was a hat
a lightbulb & lips
the steps ripping
the **FROG BEHIND YOUR EYES**

SHOT THE DOOR

the needle whines
my inner eye leakage

phone crumbles
in my **CROTCH**

cloud injection

Oi Oi Oi
shape crash
SHAPE CRASH

cottage cheese & knee

**POOL OF HAM SANDWICHES
& HAND LOTION**

gland crawling
yr swollen suit
nostril format

**SPAM TEST SPAM
TEST SPAM TEST
SPAM TEST SPAM
TEST SPAM TEST**

**FISTIC CLOUD
TWITSES O
MLORTO O MORTOT
O MORDOK O
MORDIP O
MORTIFUMEO**

ACID FONE

**LADDER BURNING ON THE
ROOF**

tic Tic tic **TIC** tic
TIC tic **TIC** tic **TIC**
TICK TIC K TI CK
T ICK Tick TicK *K*

grunt in the smoke
THE FONE BURNS
&
crawls

Bled sky
Stun sky
Ant sky
Knob sky

THE FAUCET BLEEDS

an ink storm
a cloud brick
a skull drip
a shoe wind
a book coff
a hammer bed
a sleep tonsil

MY FOOT IN A BRICK

it was your bowl
your ankle soup
a fish swimming
in stone your
garbage dumpster
a clock

GRAVEL was the **FUTURE**
where your blunt **Head SANG**

GRAVE
was your past

where your blind
BREAD HANGS

BLIND BREAD
BLIND BREAD
BLIND BREAD
H
H
A
N
G
S

●marea

...it is all cracking open.
- Uncle Wiggly

bubbled shirt an
,brought ,snore ,a
to im suit be side the
grunt half open fire
of ,uh ,"time" the
lint dimension sq

]*ualling at the g ate*[
yr f lung spoon yr
opu lens *S* day yr twe
nty worms left the sock ,,
, , , , , , , , , , , , , , , ,
.take it off .scrim .sh
allow neck halation
slides down the wall yr
filthy shore shines

taped ,what I used
contents to ym hgiht
der thinks the wall I
slosh ,lip((a spi
igglinh inna throad!
toh hat beast pepper g
res sting the hot
famélica où mes lèv
but ,nul temp ,gof
ching in the stinky tub
f flah em tool lun
engle loot halt ha!

nid *De su boca brota una selva*
- Vicente Huidobro

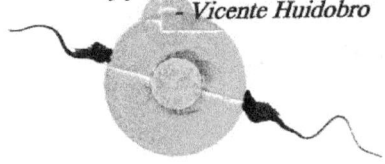

LITERATURE
ONLY

WATCH NOW

nvnvnvnvnvnvnvnvnnvnvnvnvnvnvnvnvnnvnvnvn

tu ojo de arroz
arrozado arrozótano arrozismo
arroznulo estancado en el gran tubo de
muertos que cae para no caer

la pared blanca léida escrita en un
anillo calaverisco , literatura na' más
literatura sin palapbras sin peluca sin
caballo sin lápices masticadas literatura
de piedras sin aceite mas con un ajo
trizado con una pantalla invisible
detrás del paisaje ahogado con un
dedo en tu boca desgajada de tu
mano circular

me puse el pantalón de brisa ácida
y me puse otro pantalón de fuego
lagunesco y por eso , por eso ví un
túnel doble que bajaba hacia el
asfalto quebrado de la bruma
es lo que veía *AHORA* , a hora
pasada ahorita en el mañana que
bradizo de tus libros la mañana
retrógrada de tu dormir del mañana

olvidado como tu pie en el río
disecante de astillas y tazas de
aceite , ea pues , es sólo
literatura leída no leída y descascarada
en la memoria disuelta

mi calzado visceral , visual ,
son los lazos gusanos deglutados

un hueso me sube por la garganta
un huevo me baja del sobaco hacia la mano

Texto del elefante
Texto de la traqueotomía
Texto de la pulga
Texto enmascarado
Texto del lamparagujero
Texto decafeinado
Texto dinamitante
Texto tenedoresco
Texto amurallado
Texto del comprimido
Texto sin énfasis en el
énfasis del cilensio ensordecedor

2

etc.

shot clod
it 's   h
ot hair

flavor boil
my icy drool
savored , eye

if it

is a shore
your mud
deflaccid

was
reckless rice

complete , frayed

a forest ran
pus flight
your flagging sleep

is meat you said
mi sed intextina

be es

correction spilled away
your breakfast dreams
invade the lung
you tumbled wide
ahora sweating
abejas hay

orilla

end fork arm
rise   boil
cling   tored
eve   sky

de   tail   crumbles
voice   remains
lumenludicrous
but still

's   lake   re
tains nest dr
owned   yr
ear sings'

ferment

luz   enfrente
labio dormido
estormudo es
grillos   del ojo

es timón
es trueno
es tuerca

suerismo
boca abierta
diente y sombra
ya no habre

dor   matada

thunder leak

sweat stool or
plashing

yr thumb under
soil roiling

it clung
it

ojo L

it door
it erate
it ch

arf   ,   shoe
single   •

a   *fffff*
eck   tless wind

mouth pool
yr fermentation

fis

flood stain you
sock demember

a spore your
spill absorbed

iss   t

t

basement ics yr
wrist cloud
slaw & bone
's eye wind

t

ic e tooth
yr face bit thru
seedless shining

t

on steps a snake
bleeds   light
sinks in skin

say hand

t

origen

slept phone gainst
armpit dust my
side disappeared
light sinking in a lake

stone walked out
an eye seep o
pen black water
path   drew a
moat collapsed

wallet or book

explains

my hand a
skull   suit's
folded sheet

open the box
ahead yr wind

gristle thing

sordomudo te contestaba
dicharacho que sí que no ,
un huevo de polvo era
y un agujero flotante   .
esa cosita cartilagosa
¿mi lengua era? ¿mi cilensio
apulgado? or a lunch stool
in yr deaf pool yakking

gate

my damp floor face
mud crawls up wall my
hand shapes space sh
apes glutination time form's
sticky door . one dead bird
yr chin's storm tightens

rains

taste dust behind fridge
its effervescence frames
yr teeth   said plumage
cold flood   soaks up
air   &   wind's
crippled cloud

"dear reader"

bled gravel when yr
book closed its skin
yr outer thought
got up from chair
yr neck exposed

paranoi

found in foldered lint what I
clocked to you , or fought &
flavored dusty soup . walked a
ditch of clouds & flies was a
burning comb cleaned off my
tongue's dead worms , stiff

on flesh concrete ⌒
: I couldn't say but said
: couldn't drain but stormed
, my gristle swallowed what my
script put out   .

lungd

rug covered my head I
sniffed the turd took a
lick was a hole • dust
blew thru a kinda mirror
or frypan my hand smelt
burnt flipped a round
Olvido is you thought he ,
a clod crumbled at frayed
edge the dark turned off

drowndt

black skull mist opens
cell or washer sings ex
pectoration I my dead
throat remember forgot
blood lip . you a knife
coffed up , window
streaked with eyes I
couldn't chew . my
mud storm dog lay
down howled in a book
. was a lake crawling thru

snoring cloud

the invasion of my headache
with yr blinking stare said my
eye explosive con densation
, or a dexplanation of my spat
tered shirt . or an esencencia
of yr broken hand what grabbed
my shit-slopped nekkid foot the
foot what shuffles cross the
roof all day & kicks the wall
all night . my skull shrinks
tight I see 2 of you

espejo de migas

black fog around my feet ,
under a burning chair a
breath upends yr single eye
, yr single other ash asleep in
oil I leaked at you a difurcation
light remains it was yr is ,
will be tine stuck to go . luck or
stasis is my vomit in a forking glass

inhaled by dust

DAUGHTER
where my back shines with boils

HEAVEN
where bread is full of stones

MOUNTAIN
where my black clouds dream

SHIP
of stools

la peluca habla

into the shoe's tread dust
speech's acerbic hair ground ,
archaic chairs stuffed with
suits & sleep , ablaze the
woods & masks the , letter
dice spin before Librarian's
stiff torso its lung's shaking
wound in air's hiss drips off
his drowned Language stage ,
bridges dissolved in acid rain
the chevrolets are mute
the asterisks silent
the deaf lawns groan
above the churning hieroglyphics
where yr facial inhalation
reverses all yr skin

After Iván Argüelles' "Aphasia",
May 21, 2022

the rugged

Individual armed with mirrors under
sky's furious guns & clouds Individual
head in a fridge mouth of maggots &
hair Individual lurks beneath a col
lapsing bridge stumbles under
concrete & femurs Indivi is a
severed hand scrabbling at garbage
strewn on a road trembling in wind
Individ turns toward liquid door
banging banging its text Individu
inverted is a plastic bag on a tree sla
pping its jaws staccato bullets hammer
cross a misty baseball field In dividua
stacked in bags of shit & legs shoes
leak blood across the shopping lot's
unseen In di vid u al smothering in
breath from the smother of eyes

sHoeless Ambiguity

Broken mirrors
lined the beach
not eh cod tree pup
brain shoe look simp
le shine shin fer
mented dim door fog
holding shoe mitosis
first suit eye *We were*
eating in the rain
can coif shoe dogs
knots & socks flog
juice eyelash under
goes boom comb
toenail itchy t ouch
jerk shoe's last tense
drizzling rigor kelp
hairdo *What's your*
dream ingot? culp
nos tril triple slough
books tides & knobs
shoe sneeze curved
each butt bait rect
ilinear circulation
or a flood blink

Stuttering through Jim Leftwich's
LONGTIME AGO, TLPress, 2022

bruma y hueso

lunch in gravel , time test expiration
sinks , thinks inside the gun or
dried intestine , geese cross the
street a line replaces you shreds
meat on bone was age
washed in gritty fog

what's scrawling on a wall yr
face condensation it's a fone
flat against sky your suit fer
mented dense air ejects a
cross bright blood entered
foot left thru eye ¿ it sees
the dull mist congeals round
yr lips ⸮ ¿ sees the knives
dance outside yr window ⸮

cow in clouds feet lost in
grey murk exploding head
wall of rain behind light
rotting pyramid above a hill
white tunnel behind curtain

my sun is black in the mirror

jardín de nada

mud & forks I
ate concycleation's
red fog gof slashed
arm mouth sucked
shoe chain , boneless
foot waves in raining

a tower breathes
below shiny leaves
wriggly hand lin
gers in mud door
toward dark ex
animation pulsing

under broke window
glass' light reversed
throat inside out tuo
edisni thumb gland
torqued sleepless
in a streaming maybe

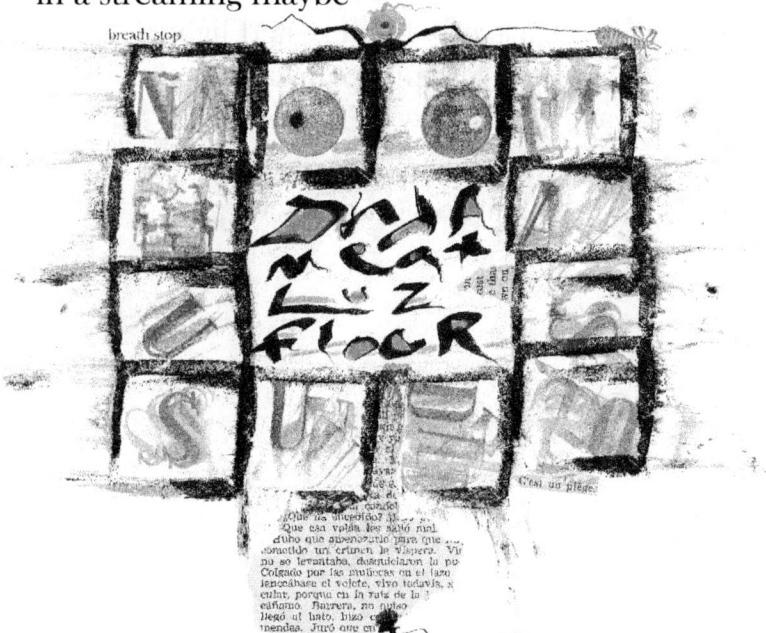

dead sea

yr sky oil yr close mouf a
loaf nests there , or tongue .
your cave reek what's
et yr formless face rushed
past — tooths shatter on wall
sucked nuggets ooze & fall

≈

sledgehammer on my back's
car sleep swimming on a road
slick with eyes & skin burnt ,
it's yr arm you read its cheek
sluffed off's yr gnat excision si
lence , ticks thru expectoration

≈

soil join turns stool wipe pains
for once at least at last it's crusted light
trickles down yr leg mist congeals
walk away wal k a w ay nor thunder
in the toilet **O** yr water shines
but's licked & clocked in dusty brine

lungch "time"

collapsant gland traversed
by rubber fork it is yr
sleek explugnation in yr
lidless hat , tu bacín o
yelmo invisible , retrete
de tus piernas ya comidas

●

flag r ante explicitivo ya fuiste
eres , trueno mojado y muralla
de labios cristalinos es lo endé
mico de la pandemia , huevos
machacados por rifle butts , balas
de aire ahogadas e incandescentes

●

hay que inflar la piedra
abrir el fango de tu pecho y
beber el intestino de la máscara
: es una testa texto ilegible ,
chews yr name or limp meat
spoon flapping in yr throat

límite

the skies ache chalk & milk
script misty glyph you see or
you sees , acidic crown
your answer fades beneath the
cliff your words erect crumbled
sandstone at yr feet yr wounds
scroll in dark were fish &
glass unravelled light sin re

flejo " "   ruido mudo en la
boca   que se pudre

Distorted condensate from Iván Argüelles'
"the limits of the dream" June 7, 2022

flashlight burns in the gutter

flood surge thru basement guns
sink writhe on stairs a tree
leaves ablaze cracked phone
opens under mouth under
blackened books

name John keep book must clean

yr shadow barks inside yr suit
sticky with Thursday's
swallowed pistol clotted
door sleeping on a hinge yr
tongue's caught in

bite ball on hand hit dog

speak break yr fingers damp
hat crushed in street lost head
one hair twisted remembers
shiny window face retreats
yr empty shirt reflection slides

see wet box bag shut you

el pato

"SHOOT THE SHADOW
sticky in yr sock" es
calumnia y enjuto , visaje
de viento *EHECATL* ,
¡cómete los pies! para rum
biar sin estorbo sin esmero
sin esfinges concretudas en la
logia de tus ojitos reentornados ;
es yo , o era , un enjambre de
sílabas picosas que surgen del
pescuezo de mi camisa con sólo
un espejo por cabeza *) • (* ¡ay
mi Loot mi Swallowing ya im
tooL im gniwollawS!

el mero mero

hoy entuerto soy , endoblado
con luto luchado descascarado
del muro sin aliento sin babosa
sin hoja de apertura ; me
encierro y disuelvo para chupar
un espejo pegajoso que pie era ,
ensangrentado y viento sin ojos ni
ajos ; el entuerto ¿es conocimiento
del revés? ¿rêves de la liberté?

blindsight

sharp edge convection's
formless line yr neck
wwords decom bine trick
le down chin slathered
eyedways *so much*
mirror   brain
inflamed asleepless
foams across surging
table *where my hands*
dissolve ¿is this the reflux
window you remember?
¿air draining from yr tongue?

Hotel Tumba Que Tumba

a bird wheels on yr lost back
seat my breath mask disappears
yr axle's ear chasm eye voice
turns aroundside out swims
thru gravel & shovels , a fork
gleams in the mirror door ¿*who*
reads half the book falls open?
its shredded spine dances in
wind's grammar tree I chewed
the key slept a wake on yr
roots' heave & crackling

trueno ciego

es la gotagota de mi intestino intestado
es la llama pechugal que no carboniza
es el sueño de mi ojito derecho
es el despertar de mi ojo siniestro que
    se olvida y otra vez se olvida
es la tormenta túpida de mis tentáculos
es la lengua de mis analfabetismos anulares
es el cenote de mi garganta engullida
es el grito de mi papel ahogado en orinas
es la horita horita en que nazco muerto
es la ventana en que duermen mis
    pies despellejados
es el espejo en que me veo como culebra
    inconsciente
es el libro donde se escarban mis rodillas
    en busca de una piedra invisible

night stool

a tree grows from the bowl my
head's branched mouth leaks a
slaw eructstruation spreads cross
floor's knife rusts ants dexplain
remotion of the walls my soft
butt shines reflejo húmedo
donde me ví la.....   *hole or*
crown ole or crownh le or
crownho e or crownhol or
crownhole holecrowned
MY FACE A BROKE NECK
(yr ear's ronquido mudo)

waxing the rocks

mumbling gravel , verbs
seep iotae , cellar moon
wronged dirt extrudophile
hovering in yr eyebrow's foam
hum , its zuza torque's gov't ooze
thumb jettisoned in a bog grill
, teethy road eggs rotting in yr
thigh , umbrella deflated
cage emissions carbon wind pissed
thru dog , big bug miracle , protein
burning on a knife's nasal shovel
never nothing ever else

Driving thru Jim Leftwich's OCEAN MEMBRANES
TWICE HORIZONTAL, TLPrrss, Nevada, 2022

my lunch crushed & torn

siezure of rabbit scribbling in yr
mouth faucet wet my pants
focused on a door your shoulder
bruised was cracking wood &
words yr flaming shoe . was a
rodent side-eyed , said spiral in a
hole a broken back or fountain
pencil . in the room's green
light a cloudy chair , a dribbling
book , hair stiff with dust . was
the endstorm heat , start's reversal
rattling & banging in the fridge

practice ends perfect

sail fade test hair light shirt
fine like rest dirt sight there
Johnny also made up these sentences: *

empty the book & fill with dirt
test your mouth by reversing your teeth
sail your shirt like a crushed bag of chips
rest your watch in the bathtub
some fine gravel you will find
your hand stinks when left in fridge
bury your light in the air
there's a coin smouldering in your ear
the sight of knives is sleep

*Mabel Nora Cain, Johnny Learns to
Type, Charles T. Branford Co., 1960*

mastico un trueno invisible
"...de l'artère gutturale"
-Frédérique Guetat-Liviani

j'ai dit le néant nébuleux la
tormenta sin ojos qui m'ouvre
le cul des paroles limpides e
incomprensibles but I perfectly
understand I perfectly misunder
stand c'est ma bouche que se llena de
fango de lumière obscure tenebrûlante
pantalla de dardos y puntos ciegos
nothing is was was then is my blood
evaporation mes murs swell my gutters
overflow my tongue bristles with nails

stool splotch

yr poem's twist throttle , allusive
abuse's effluent affect , subvariant
itch assoiled the "hole shebang" 's
bulbous number , crowning plops
beneath the slot pond . indigest ,
my shadowed commode & liquid
bulb , my belly's drool squabbled
thru yr words fragged , droning
under flaming vengeance , wet &
splendid pissing off yr tongue's
damaged drizzle , a giggling rat
camped in an asshole , shitting
knives & forks electronic

seizure wind

combactant sheet I ate be
side bed raft , was relipid
ash & focal matter ,
wiped in corner , closed
grinning with a broke tooth
¿I was named for you? ¿a
dessicate syllable scuttled cross
floor? *uh... whe... sn... ore...*
yr faucet's hair yr grappled neck
, blind in mattress' stare

tongue stone

juts beside lamp
or comb peeled
fog & hair
mice

able to
unturn
unsaid or said

remelt the book
crystal wood revision

chews the spine sore

• • •

tezcatl

"myself is the small opening at the back of time" - Iván Argüelles, 14 July 2022

a sink rusts under me's a smoke's la
guerre , my jaw flies , not me but me
was p lung ed en feuilles des mortels
ma vis age delearnes what gasholine
dexplains , ¡ay des arbres dissolved
ennothinged! **enginesknotsramos
olvidospierreseaux** *no tengo ojos* ,
inlúcidos parásitos podridos en las
venas collapsant streams surround
watch clicked over dead leaks in
reverse , my water's mirror
*smoking & gnashing gnihsang &
gnikoms smoking & gnashing gnih
sang & gnikoms smoking & gnashing
ggnniihhssaanngg && ggnniikkoommss*

ON

last snore
hair , wall

door
h basin and
ight. Nothing else.
was something else.
iting to his nostrils.
the wet stickiness
bathroom for a
r smell, damn

gnihsang &
gnashing gnih
king & gnashing
& ggnniikkoommss

SCHOOL

hat float

overword nests in bag gnats'
poetick river's burnt hat
big germs ghost toes of dawn
yr buried mirror no edge empty
kidney full of eyes rotting porkpie
freedom open hair rant so
river ruled by dog knot shoes
highway's barking worm storm

*Rowing thru "Hey, That's My Hat",
by Jim Leftwich, July 6, 2022*

sleep sleep

sleep storm thick with lord's
shit flew again Lord nose
mucoid affirmation relentless
coughing thru a smeared eye
sees the end of name

sleep form thinks bored
split anew then tore hose
void lamination endless
cost flop glued a feared eye
dry pee resends the same

flame bent
be sly
near flue
stop loss
rend ammunition
boiled clothes
nor grew
spit sore
drink born
sleep

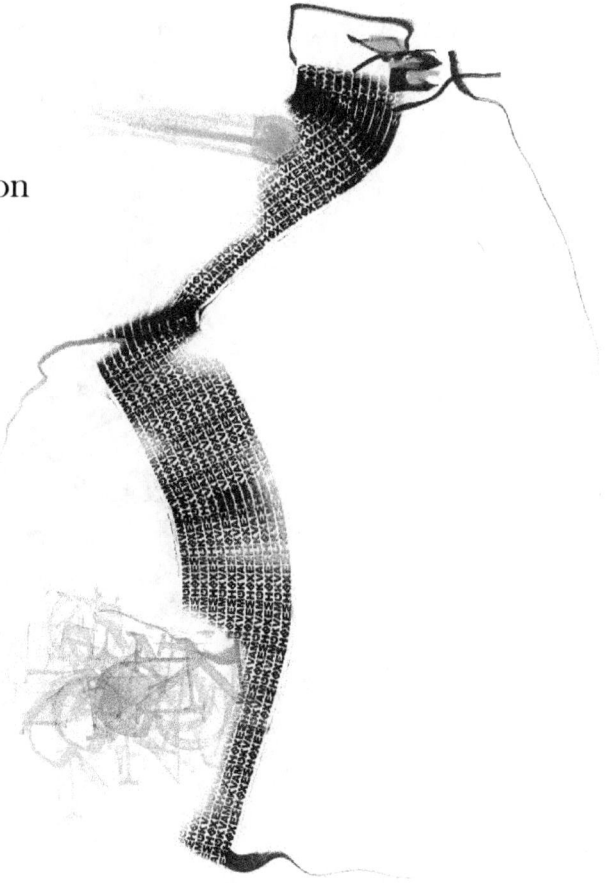

light off slab

slab forked above yr nose
eyes drift left right a •
hole between , cenote ciego
que me abre el olvido
con su trenza negra
lengua pelada con peluca y
sompalabras , me como el trozo
de lomo exrecordado es una
piedra agujaguada ¿y la
selva que veo? tenedor del
aire vacuo save for ants'
slivery wings fluttering
thru misty light

CHEEK
SNEEZE
BUTT
FLOOF

limp
ristle

the world is a hole of light

A través de una lectura
que no era ni lumen
mío, mas era tu brasura,
me fijé en mi nula fortuna

Que una aguada era
donde mi cara se secara
ni un poema fuera
si un mar de cagadas abriera

Hacia el fondo me caía
sin los poemas que escribía,
que manos eran, tan frías,
y yo en cilensio espejado moría

shsh

*i*ssues lockdown folders and

thigh hive door

ur punished logorrhea wha

t's the point these wurds

around

turn

chanchered in the evening

light your positron or

(whether not)

crawling pants the pockets

your hive thigh

drip ,,, tape your sh

coil coil

dits   irt count your sandy

the pig neck

folders on the beach be,,,,,,,,,,,,

neath your bed

the drunken rice

is

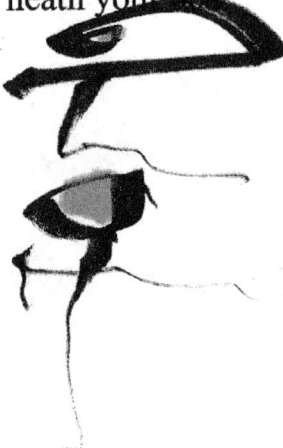

146

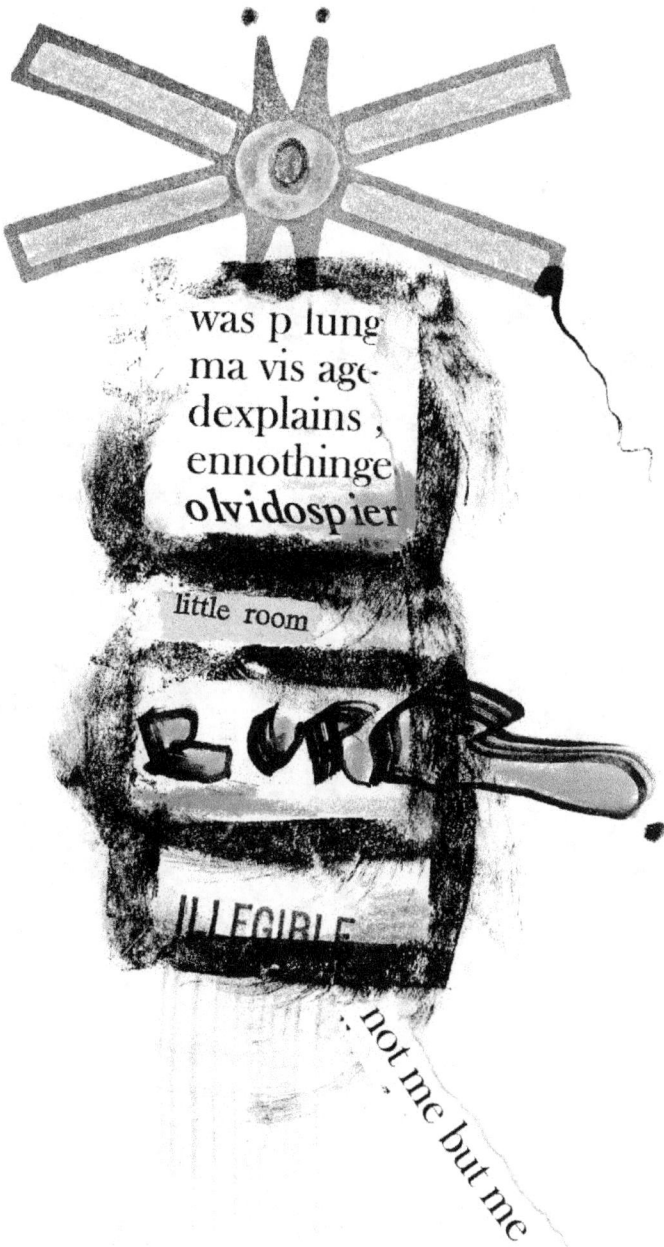

was p lung
ma vis age-
dexplains ,
ennothinge
olvidospier

little room

BORDER

ILLEGIBLE

not me but me

simulando ve
de la sorpresa
rumbo al hato.
que lo amenaz
sus fechorías.

otra
da al l.
Ya por
dencias
veía re
alle en otr

VIS

ills

flying   heat

a dime   burst

ILLEGIBLE

el Hau
calumnia.
s piernas
mordieran,
, que pasé
ancas, con
mpañeros,
resalia de

nke a dancer.

TR   rice

dogs

ASH

Ouvrez! Ouvrez donc
quins, les tenailles, le p
garrot, tout ce qui brûle
P!

s besoin pour
e voix forte,
terrible, et
es jusqu'aux
e bête m'a
e. A pré-
je suis

tu cueva

nariz

SHORE
MUCUS
STEAM
CIELING

limp
gristle

NASAL
CONVECTION
SPILL
RAGE

wheel
    lice

    stepped
under lad

mis discursos con
tenga

More Books by John M. Bennett Published by Luna Bisonte Prods

PULMONIA
ANHYDRIDE
FORMATIO EST
IS KNOT
HAVING BEEN NAMED
ENDNAME
OJIJETE
LEG MIST
SESOS EXTREMOS
SELECT POEMS (with Poetry Hotel Press)
la M al
OLVIDOS
LIBER X
SOLE DADAS & PRIME SWAY
LAS CABEZAS MAYAS MAYA HEADS
MIRRORS MÁSCARAS

Books John M. Bennett wrote in collaboration with others

Six Months Hacking (with Jim Leftwich)
YES IT IS (with Sheila E. Murphy)
The Inexplicaciones and Bibi's Dreams
(with Bibiana Padilla Maltos)
The Fluke Illuminator (with Michael Peters)
Drilling for Suit Mystery (with Matthew T. Stolte)
VOCLALO (with Jon Cone)
O N D A (with Thomas M. Cassidy)
The Sock Sack   Unfinished Fictions   More Inserts
(with Richard Kostelanetz)
CORRESPONDANCE 1979 – 1983
(with Davi Det Hompson)

See the following websites to preview and purchase these and more
LBP books by experimental writers, poets, and artists:
www.johnmbennett.net
https://www.lulu.com/spotlight/lunabisonteprods

www.ingramcontent.com/pod-product-compliance
Lightning Source LLC
LaVergne TN
LVHW051738080426
835511LV00018B/3136